Fifty Hikes in Connecticut

Overlooking Merimere Reservoir from West Peak

FIFTY HIKES IN CONNECTICUT

A Guide to Short Walks and Day Hikes Around the Nutmeg State

GERRY AND SUE HARDY

Photographs by the Authors

Backcountry Publications
Woodstock, VT

Acknowledgments

Many of our thoughts were honed on our numerous hiking companions, to whom we are very grateful. The Appalachian Mountain Club groups we hike with provide an endless supply of wit and good fellowship.

Above all, we would like to thank the dedicated chairmen of the Connecticut Forest and Park Association for the existence and maintenance of Connecticut's Blue Trails, members of the Connecticut Chapter of the AMC for maintaining the Appalachian Trail in Connecticut, and all those who laid out and maintain the many other fine trails in our state.

We would also like to thank our editor Cathy Baker for her help and encouragement.

An Invitation to the Reader

If you find that conditions have changed along these trails, please let the authors and publisher know so that corrections may be made in future editions. Address all correspondence:
Editor, *50 Hikes*
Backcountry Publications
Woodstock, VT 05091

Photo Credits

Photographs on pages 19, 25, 31, 61, 99, 115, and 144 by Nancy-Jane Jackson; photographs on pages 34 and 42 by Lawrence S. Millard. All other photographs by the authors.

ISBN hardbound: 0-912274-90-5
ISBN softbound: 0-942440-05-6
Library of Congress Catalog Card Number: 77-94006
©1978 by Gerry and Sue Hardy
Printed in the United States of America
All rights reserved
Designed by Wladislaw Finne

To David, Mary Anne,
Charlie, and Patty—
with love.

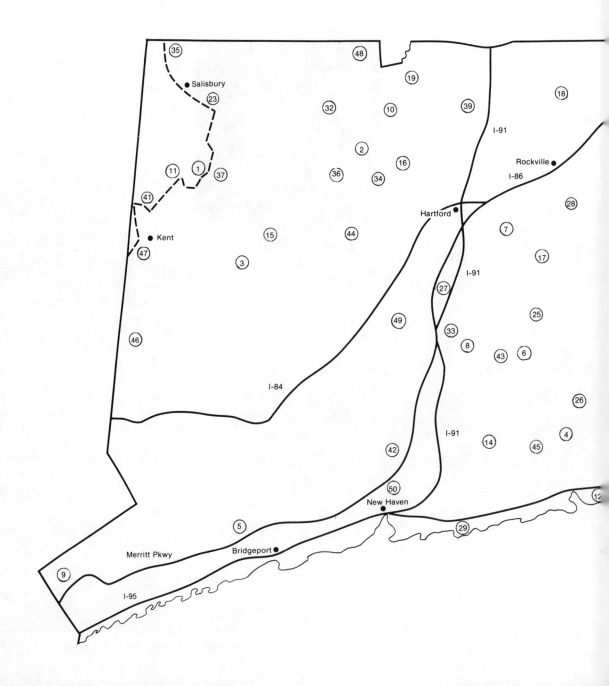

㉟ 35

● Salisbury

㉓ 23

⑪ 11 ① 1 ㊲ 37

㊶ 41

● Kent

㊼ 47

③ 3

㊻ 46

I-84

⑮ 15

㉟ 48

⑲ 19

㉜ 32 ⑩ 10 ㊴ 39

② 2 ⑯ 16

㊱ 36 ㉞ 34

⑱ 18

I-91

● Rockville

I-86

㊹ 44

Hartford ●

㉘ 28

⑦ 7

⑰ 17

㉗ 27

I-91

㊾ 49

㉝ 33

⑧ 8

㉕ 25

㊸ 43 ⑥ 6

㉖ 26

㊷ 42

I-91

⑭ 14

④ 4

㊺ 45

㊿ 50

New Haven ●

⑤ 5

㉙ 29

⑫ 12

Merritt Pkwy

Bridgeport ●

⑨ 9

I-95

Contents

Willimantic

Connecticut Tpke

Norwich

I-95

New London

22 31 21 38 20 24 40 30 13

Fifty Hikes in Connecticut

Introduction

Contrary to popular opinion, Connecticut is not all city and suburbs. A gratifyingly high proportion of our state's woodland is preserved as state parks and state forests. In fact, the only state in New England with more miles of hiking trails is New Hampshire.

These fifty hikes represent all areas of the state and traverse almost all the existing natural habitats. Naturally, this selection is only a sampler and, of necessity, somewhat reflects our own preferences and prejudices. We chose the hikes with an eye to the hiking family; most are suitable for families with young children (who are usually far more capable physically than psychologically). But remember, a hike adults and teenagers can cover in four hours may take all day with youngsters along, especially if they take time to examine their surroundings closely.

We have written this book to please both the armchair hiker and the trail walker by fleshing out directions with photographs and snippets of natural history. We have also tried to answer some of the questions the average hiker might ask while walking these trails. The phenomena we describe we actually saw on these fifty hikes; by being fairly observant you can see the same things. For this reason our descriptions

The Windsor Locks Canal

are short on wildlife, which is seen only occasionally, and long on vegetation and terrain. Effective observation of animal life requires very slow movement (if any), blinds, and binoculars or scopes. In contrast, vegetation and terrain features require only an alert eye and an inquiring mind.

These hikes, which we feel represent some of the most attractive of the state's trails, break longer trails into palatable chunks that can be completed in a specified period of time. In addition to some of the best pieces of the Blue Trail system, finest stretches of Connecticut's section of the Appalachian Trail (AT), and more interesting state park trail systems, we have included a few hikes in wildlife sanctuaries and city- and town-owned, open-space areas.

Choosing a Hike

The hikes are presented in order of their overall difficulty; the first hike, Cathedral Pines, is the easiest, and the last one, Regicides Trail, the most difficult. However, since difficulty is averaged over an entire hike, many of the later hikes have quite easy sections. The book is broken into two parts for your convenience: half-day hikes and all-day hikes. While the half-day hikes can be completed by many hikers in three hours or less, trying to

complete an all-day hike in an afternoon may cause you to miss supper.

Total distance is the mileage walked if you complete the entire hike as described. Many of these hikes lend themselves readily to shortening if you desire an easier day. Trail distances are given in fractions of a mile for some hikes and in decimals for others. Fractional distances are estimates, while decimal distances have usually been measured with a wheel and are quite accurate.

Hiking time is computed from a simple formula used all over the country: two miles an hour plus one-half hour for every 1,000 feet of vertical rise. Thus, a six-mile hike on flat terrain would have a three-hour hiking time, but a six-mile hike with 2,000 feet of climbing would take four hours. If you are middle-aged and a beginning hiker you probably won't match "book time" for a while. A young, experienced hiker will consistently better these times. One word of caution—hiking time means just that and does not allow for lunch stops, rest stops, sightseeing, or picture taking.

The *rating* for each hike refers to the average difficulty of the terrain you traverse on the route we have described. The difficulty of a hike is relative. A tough section in Connecticut is far easier than a tough section in New

Hampshire or Vermont. Our rating system is the one used by the Connecticut Chapter of the Appalachian Mountain Club and is designed for Connecticut trails. It combines such factors as elevation gain, rock scrambling, footpath condition, and steepness. Hikes rated D are the easiest and A the most difficult. The seven categories used in our rating system are:

D.   Flat terrain; little or no elevation change, easy footing
CD.   Intermediate between C and D
C.   Average terrain; moderate ups-and-downs with some need to watch footing
CB.   Intermediate between C and B
B.   Difficult terrain; steep climbs, considerable elevation gain or some poor footing or both
AB.   Intermediate between A and B
A.   Very tough terrain; maximum elevation gain, poor footing or hand-assisted scrambling up steep pitches or both

When selecting a day's ramble, don't overdo it. If you haven't hiked before, try the shorter, easier hikes first and build up to the longer ones gradually. Don't bite off more than you can chew—that takes all the pleasure out of hiking. As the saying goes, "walk till you're half tired out, then turn around and walk back."

Highlights are not just teasers to attract you to a particular hike. Used properly they should help you choose a hike on the basis of weather and the proclivities of your companions. On clear, cool days distant viewpoints are in order. Youngsters like nature museums, scrambling over rocks, and swimming. Hot days call for cool, flat, woods walks.

The sketch maps accompanying the hikes are based on trail or topographic maps. They are meant to give you an idea of the route you are to follow and include only key landmarks.

About Connecticut Seasons

Hiking in Connecticut is a four-season avocation. Our winters are relatively mild—we rarely have temperatures below zero Fahrenheit or snow accumulations over a foot. In general, the snow deepens and the temperature drops as you travel north and west. Often the southeastern part of the state is snow-free much of the winter and is the first area in the state to experience spring.

Spring is usually wet and muddy, although there is frequently a dry period of high fire danger before the trees leaf out. Spring flowers start in April and peak in May. Days of extreme heat in the nineties can come anytime in late spring.

The humid heat of summer demands short, easy, early morning strolls. Beginners often think summer is the best time to hike; veterans consider it the worst time! However, in summer the foliage is lush and botanizing is at its best.

Fall is the ideal hiking season. Cool, crisp days make us forget the enervating heat of summer; the colorful foliage and clear air make New England's fall unsurpassed. A better combination of season and place may exist elsewhere, but we doubt it. The color starts with a few shrubs and the bright reds of swamp maples. When other trees start to turn, the swamp maples are bare. Then tree follows tree—sugar maple, ash, birch, beech, and finally oak—turning, blending, fading, falling. There is no better way to enjoy a New England fall than to explore the woods on foot.

How to Hike

We do not mean to tell you how to walk. Most of us have been walking from an early age. Rather, we offer a few hints to help you gain as much pleasure and satisfaction as possible from a hike.

First and most important, wear decent, comfortable footgear that is well broken in. Children can often hike comfortably in good sneakers; adults usually shouldn't. We're heavier and our feet need more support than canvas offers. On the other hand, you don't need heavyweight mountain boots in Connecticut. A lightweight hiking boot or a good workboot with a vibram or lug sole is ideal. While these soles may be hard on the woods trails, we do recommend them as most Connecticut hiking alternates between woods and rocky ledges, where the lug soles are very helpful. Your boots should be worn over two pairs of socks, one lightweight and one heavyweight. Wool is preferable for both pairs as it provides warmth even when wet.

Second, wear comfortable, loose-fitting clothes that don't bind, bunch, or chafe. Cotton T-shirts are good; synthetics are less comfortable. For our day hikes, except in winter, we favor cut-off jeans or good hiking shorts; they're loose and have lovely pockets for storing a neckerchief, a handkerchief, insect repellent, film, tissues, and a pocket knife.

Establish a comfortable pace that you can maintain for long periods of time. The hiker who charges down the trail not only

misses the subtleties of the surroundings but also frequently starts gasping for breath after fifteen minutes or so of hiking. That's no fun! A steady pace lets you see more and cover more ground comfortably than the start-and-stop, huff-and-puff hiker.

When you climb a slope, slow your pace so you can continue to the top without having to stop. (Having to stop is different from choosing to stop at places of interest!) With practice you'll develop an uphill rhythm and find you actually cover ground faster by going slowly.

Many veteran hikers use a restful step in which they lock the knee the weight is on, letting the other leg rest as it swings relaxed from the hip to take the next step. This way each leg rests half the time. An hour of hiking is thus much less tiring than an hour of standing, where neither leg gets to rest.

What to Carry

You may have read articles on the portable household the backpacker carries. While the day hiker needn't shoulder this burden, there are some things you should carry to assure a comfortable and safe hike. Ideally you will always carry your emergency gear and never use it. Items 2-10 below live in our day packs:

1. Small, comfortable, lightweight pack.
2. First-aid kit containing at least adhesive bandages, moleskin (for incipient blisters), scissors, adhesive tape, gauze pads, aspirin, salt tablets, ace bandage, and bacitracin. We always carry both elastic knee and ankle braces—we have used them more than any of our other first-aid equipment.
3. Wool shirt or sweater and a lightweight, nylon windbreaker. A fast-moving cold front can turn a balmy spring day into a blustery snow-spitting disaster, and sun-warmed, sheltered valleys may contrast sharply with elevated open ledges.
4. Lightweight raingear. In warm, rainy weather, hikers are of two minds about raingear—some don it immediately and get wet from perspiration; other don't and get wet from the rain. In colder weather wear it for warmth. In any case, if the day is threatening it's wise to have dry clothes in the car.
5. Water. Except for occasional springs, water in southern New England is rarely safe to drink. Always carry at least a quart canteen (more on hot summer days) per hiker.
6. Food. In addition to your lunch, carry some high-energy food for emergencies. Gorp—a hand-mixed combination of chocolate chips, nuts, and dried fruit—is good.
7. Flashlight with extra batteries and bulb. You should plan to return to your car before dark, but be prepared in case you're delayed.
8. A well-sharpened pocket knife. This tool has a thousand uses.
9. Map and compass (optional). These items are not necessary for day hikers in Connecticut who stay on well-defined trails and use a guidebook. However, if you want to do any off-trail exploring, you should learn to use a map and compass and carry them with you.
10. Others: toilet paper (always); insect repellent (in season); a hat or sunscreen lotion (on bright days); a wool hat and gloves (in spring and fall).

Winter hiking requires much additional equipment and does not fall within the scope of this book. Nonetheless, it is a lovely time to hike and we would encourage you to hone your skill in mild weather, consult experienced winter hikers, and consider winter's clear, crisp, often snow-white days.

Potpourri

Footing is the major difference between road walking and hiking. Roads present a minimum of obstacles to trip you; at times hiking trails seem to have a

Day packs showing the Connecticut 400 Patch

maximum. The angular traprock cobbles on many of Connecticut's ridges tend to roll beneath your feet, endangering ankles and balance. An exposed wet root acts as a super banana peel and lichen on wet rock as a lubricant. Stubs of improperly cut bushes are nearly invisible obstacles which trip or puncture. All these potential hazards dictate that you walk carefully on the trail.

It is far safer to hike with a companion than to venture out alone. Should an accident occur while you're alone, you're in trouble. If you must hike alone, be sure someone knows where you are, your exact route, and when you plan to return.

While hiking, don't litter. The AMC motto "Carry In-Carry Out"

is a good one. Carry a small plastic bag in your pack for garbage. When it comes to human waste, head well off the trail and stay at least two hundred feet from any water. Be sure to bury any wastes and toilet paper. Leave the woods as you found them.

On any hike, the vegetation you see has been left unpicked by previous trekkers. You, in turn, should leave all plants for the next hiker to admire. This courtesy applies not only to the wanton picker, but also to the scientific collector. If you must collect, do it away from the trails and off state land. Remember to "take only pictures; leave only footprints."

Connecticut has a limited-liability law to protect landowners who grant access to the general

public free of charge. This saves property owners from capricious lawsuits and opens up more private lands for trails.

Hiking should be much more than a walk in the woods. Knowledge of natural and local history adds another dimension to your rambles. We dip lightly into these areas to give you a sampling to whet an inquiring mind. To aid further investigation, we offer this short descriptive bibliography. Good field guides in your pack will add immeasurably to a hike.

Connecticut Walk Book. Definitive guidebook to the entire Blue Trail system. Published by the Connecticut Forest and Parks Association, 1010 Main St., East Hartford, CT 06108.

The Appalachian Trail Guide to Connecticut and Massachusetts. One of the series of guidebooks to the 2,025-mile Appalachian Trail. Published by the Appalachian Trail Conference, P.O. Box 236, Harper's Ferry, WV 25425.

Topographical Maps. Detailed maps showing contour lines, elevation, streams, roads, etc. Available from U.S. Geological Survey, 1200 South Eads St., Arlington, VA 22202.

Birds of North America. Excellent beginner's guide. Published by Golden Press, New York, 1966.

The Peterson Field Guide

Series. Definitive volumes on insects, birds, flowers, animal tracks, trees and shrubs, etc. Published by Houghton Mifflin Company, Boston.

A Guide to New England's Landscape. Fine natural history descriptions with locations of specific examples by Neil Jorgensen. Revised edition published by Pequot Press, Chester, CT.

Be Expert with Map and Compass. An introduction to orienteering by Bjorn Kjellstrom. Published by Charles Scribner's Sons, New York, 1967.

Connecticut: A Guide to its Roads, Lore, and People. The Federal Writer's Project's excellent compact history and travel guide to Connecticut. Available at most local libraries.

Backpacking: One Step at a Time. An interesting discussion of hiking and full of nuggets of information by Harvey Manning. Published by Vintage Books, Random House, New York, 1973.

The New Complete Walker. Definitely the hiker's bible, by Colin Fletcher. Published by Alfred A. Knopf, Inc., New York, 1976.

For a good Connecticut road map drop a card to Connecticut Department of Transportation, Bureau of Highways, P.O. Drawer A, Wethersfield, CT 06109.

The Connecticut 400 Club

Many hikers collect attractive patches to signify completion of a goal. The AMC sponsors, among others, the New Hampshire 4000-Footers Club and the New England 4000-Footers Club for those who have climbed the forty-seven mountains in New Hampshire or the sixty-four in northern New England that are over 4,000 feet high. Special patches are awarded to applicants for a small fee.

Connecticut's peaks are less lofty. However, the Connecticut Chapter of the AMC has since 1976 sponsored the Connecticut 400 Club whose members have hiked all the "Through Trails" (approximately 450 miles) described in the *Connecticut Walk Book*. Patches are awarded to applicants for a small fee. The Connecticut 400 Club was established not only to recognize those who have hiked the through trails but, perhaps more importantly, to encourage hikers to explore all the trails in the state, thus reducing traffic on the famous but overused Appalachian Trail.

For the name and address of the current Connecticut 400 Patch chairman or for information on the Connecticut Chapter of the AMC, write to the Appalachian Mountain Club, 5 Joy St., Boston, MA 02108.

Half-Day Hikes

1 Cathedral Pines

Total distance: .6 mile
Hiking time: ½ hour / Rating: C
Highlights: Impressive white pine grove

Hiking the AT in Cathedral Pines

This first hike breaks our general rule that the trips in this book should be true hikes. However, this short walk on a section of the famous Appalachian Trail takes you through a very special place. The Cathedral Pines are impressive in a hushed, humbling way; naturalists talk about this stand in the same awed tones that historians use to describe the great Gothic cathedrals of Europe.

To reach the pine grove, follow CT 4 west .5 mile from its junction with CT 125 in Cornwall. Turn left on Bolton Hill Road, which forks immediately, and then proceed right on Jewell Street. Shortly, at the next fork, go left .2 mile to the white blazes that mark the trail. A pull-out on the left a few yards past the blazes provides room to park.

The flavor of this area is apparent even from your car. Two-hundred-year-old pines, 3 feet or more in diameter and reaching 150 feet in height, tower over the road. When New Hampshire's virgin Pisgah Tract was leveled by the great hurricane of 1938, this stand of second-growth pine became New England's finest.

Since white pines are not part of the climax forest, they were probably relatively rare in colonial times. With the westward migration of the New England farmer, these pines filled in abandoned fields and became a valuable timber crop. The soft, durable wood made it the East's most important conifer, and it was commonly planted in stately stands. Since 1938, when the hurricane downed thousands of acres of managed white pine forest, this type of silviculture has been practiced less freqently.

A slightly smaller picturesque pine perches on a boulder by the roadside. While it is probably as old as the ones surrounding it, the struggle for sustenance on this barren rock has stunted its growth.

From your car walk the few yards back downhill to the white blazes and turn right into the magnificent woods. This forty-two acre stand of pines is owned by the Nature Conservancy, a national organization that has preserved over ten thousand acres in Connecticut alone.

You are entering a forest where nature has been allowed to run her course—an unmanaged woodland. Dead and dying trees are scattered throughout and fallen hulks dot the hillside. Woodpeckers inadvertently defend the standing forest by eating the grubs, carpenter ants, and various beetles that feast on the living trees; below, decomposers work on fallen trees to create new soil.

As you progress uphill, you see a few great hemlocks among the tall pines. Only young hemlocks grow in the understory; unlike the sun-loving pine, the hemlock tolerates shade and can thus replace itself. If the natural succession remains undisturbed here for a few more centuries, the hemlock will take over from the pines to form a self-perpetuating climax forest.

Many of the fallen logs are havens for the common red-backed salamander. Most salamanders need water nearby to breed, but the female of this species curls around the eggs, protecting them until they hatch. The logs provide a moist environment, shade, and an abundance of insect life to feed on. Be sure that you carefully replace any logs you turn over so the damp earth needed by so many creatures remains protected.

As you near the top of the hill, the pines thin out and shrink in size. Here, where there is less shade, the undergrowth is thicker. Note the large pileated woodpecker holes high on the side of the great white pine on your left. Just under .2 mile from the start, you reach a woods road, which you follow gently downhill until you sight a tar road. Turn around and retrace your steps to your car.

2 Great Pond

Total distance: 1½ miles
Hiking time: ¾ hour / Rating: D
Highlights: Quiet pond

This hike circles a delightful little body of water paradoxically called Great Pond. You appreciate short hikes such as this one best when you take them slowly. Adopt a silent hesitation step to enhance your chances of surprising wildlife. Be the first out on a summer Sunday morning and increase your chances even more.

From the junction of CT 167 and US 202 in Simsbury, follow CT 167 west .2 mile to Firetown Road and turn right. Proceed down this road for .7 mile and then fork left onto Great Pond Road. The dirt entrance road to Great Pond State Forest is on the right in 1.6 miles. After passing an outdoor chapel frequently used for weddings, the road ends in a parking lot.

We owe the preservation of this 280-acre state forest to James L. Goodwin, the forester and conservationist who established a tree nursery here in 1932. Twenty-four years later, the nursery was designated Connecticut Tree Farm Number One. The land was subsequently bequeathed to the state by Mr. Goodwin and was dedicated as a state forest in 1967.

Many trails crisscross by the parking lot. This hike starts at

Great Pond through the trees

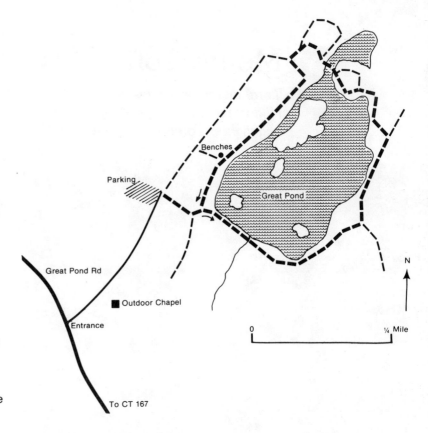

the far right corner of the lot on the wide, well-worn, horseshoe-pocked trail through the pine grove. The pines are so dense in this spot that no new ones have sprouted despite the millions of seeds shed annually by opening cones. Instead, the main under-story tree is the shade-tolerant hemlock. In early summer, pink lady-slippers add color to the soft carpet of pine needles.

Walk past a trail that leaves on the right, and soon, with the pond visible through the trees, you reach a junction. Turn right at this intersection, but from here on always bear left until you have completed the circuit around the pond and returned to this spot. Following this rule of thumb, you may take an oc-casional dead end to the water's edge—never mind, for these in-advertent side trips allow you to admire the pond from many dif-ferent viewpoints.

Shallow Great Pond is strewn with lily pads and bordered with emergent vegetation and tree stumps gnawed by beavers. The moisture-loving royal fern stands on water-girt hummocks and even grows in shallow water. Dragonflies dance around and light with all four wings out-spread. Iridescent damselflies flap awkwardly and then perch with wings clasped together above a long, thin abdomen.

From numerous spots you can see the pine-dotted islands rising from the pond's northern end.

Just before you reach a small boardwalk you come to a black birch trying out its "stilts." It sprouted on a stump that is slowly rotting away; its spread-eagle roots are assuming more and more of the burden. Some day, with the stump gone, this tree will stand alone on braced roots. The boardwalk and the plank footbridge ahead provide a dry-shod, close-up view of the lush swamp vegetation.

Beyond the bridge, we froze at the sight of a large doe feeding in a clearing. Moving only when she lowered her head to feed and freezing during her periodic surveillances, we came within thirty yards of her before our suspicious forms elicited a steady stare. Mosquitoes feeding happily on our unmoving forms finally forced us to move. Her instant flight was punctuated by the white flag of her upraised tail.

Near the end of the hike a pair of benches at trailside invite you to blend into the scenery. As you sit quietly, the many and varied bird calls become more ap-parent—and are freqently in-terrupted by the saucy chatter of the conifer-loving red squir-rel. You complete the loop around Great Pond a short dis-tance beyond the benches. The next trail right returns you to your car.

3 Mount Tom Tower

Total distance: 1½ miles
Hiking time: 1 hour/Rating: C
Highlights: Tower views, state park

Stone chimney on Mt. Tom

Though short, this is a rewarding half-day hike. By using the swimming and picnicking facilities you can profitably spend the whole day. The tree-topping tower on the mountain offers a full 360-degree view of the surrounding countryside.

Mount Tom State Park is located just off US 202 southwest of Litchfield, 1 mile east of its junction with CT 341. Watch for the state park sign by the access road (Old Town Road). Once inside the 233-acre park (a fee is charged on summer weekends), follow the one-way signs to a junction with a sign that directs you right to the tower trail. Park in the picnic area.

Take the white-blazed trail straight up a steep gravel road (no vehicles allowed). Silver birches and red oaks predominate on this slope. In early spring you will see the white blossoms of the shadbush (or juneberry), so named because it flowers about the time shad run up the rivers. This shrub with light gray bark is less noticeable in other seasons. The juicy berries, which ripen in June, are edible and taste not unlike huckleberries. Indians used to dry and compress them into great loaves, chunks of which were broken off

Mt Tom Pond

Beach

To US 202

Old Town Rd

Parking

N

Mt Tom

0   ¼ Mile

over the winter for use as a sweetener.

In ¾ mile the trail ends at the base of a circular stone tower thirty-four feet high. Wood stairs inside lead you to a cement roof — watch your head as you emerge.

Below is spring-fed Mount Tom Pond with its bathhouses and sand beaches. Beyond Mount Tom Pond to the northwest you see the Riga Plateau with (from left to right) Mounts Bear (see Hike 35), Race, and Everett. To the right of the plateau and beyond Bantam Lake, a popular boating and fishing spot, white church spires mark the historic town of Litchfield. Toward the southwest the rugged hills blend into New York's Harriman Park. On very clear days you can see Long Island Sound to the south with the outskirts of New York City at right.

To return by a different route, follow the white blazes back down, but at the second level, grassy area turn right onto a rocky path. Although there are no blazes along this rough descent, you should have no trouble following the well-worn treadway.

Near the bottom, as you approach a gravel road, you pass a handsome stone chimney and fireplace with nearby cement foundations. Their origin is unknown to us. Follow the gravel

road to the left until it turns left; now take the path that branches right downhill. Log steps embedded in the slope lead to a tar road.

At this park in mid-April, we encountered our first black flies of the season. Three biting insects are dominant in Connecticut. Black flies, which actually take a chunk out of you, are first. Mercifully, as repellents rarely bother them, they need well-oxygenated running water to breed in so their season is short here. Mosquitoes, which breed in stagnant water, come next; good repellents usually work well with them. Later in the spring deer

flies arrive, hovering around the back or your head waiting for a chance to land and dig in. You can usually kill them as they alight; fortunately they rarely occur in great numbers, so by paying attention you can reduce your personal cloud of these pests with great satisfaction.

When you reach the tar road, turn left. Shortly another road left takes you to the picnic area. As we stood by the car discussing this hike, a pileated woodpecker, red-crested with white underwings, flew overhead. This uncommon bird, nearly as large as a crow, is the drummer that excavates great rectangular holes in unsound trees to reach nests of carpenter ants.

4 Gillette Castle

Total distance: 2 miles
Hiking time: 1¼ hours/Rating: CD
Highlights: River views, castle

Gillette Castle

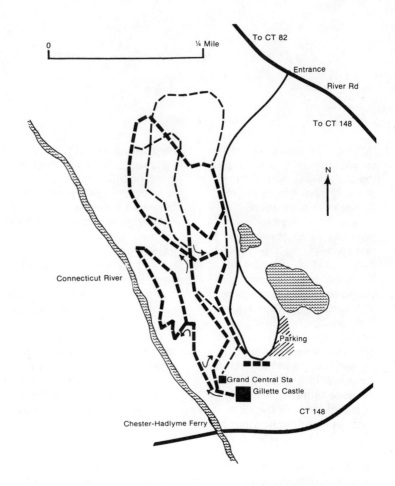

Most hikes in this book take you into areas where the pedestrian attractions far exceed those that you can see from your car. Gillette Castle is an exception. A visit to this eccentric structure provides a grand excuse to explore by road the picturesque Haddam-Lyme countryside around it and to indulge in a short ferry ride. The two state-maintained ferries across the Connecticut River harken back to the days of a more leisurely pace and are a fit transition to this area with its turn-of-the-century aura.

If you're starting west of the Connecticut River, come over on the Chester-Hadlyme ferry (CT 148), which offloads a few miles from the castle, and return on the South Glastonbury-Rocky Hill run about 25 miles north on CT 160. (Both ferries cross at regular intervals and charge a nominal fee.) From the Chester-Hadlyme ferry continue east on CT 148 to River Road, on the left. If you're starting east of the river, take CT 148 west out of Hadlyme and turn right onto River Road. (From this direction you must plan a detour to make the ferry crossing.) Follow the signs on River Road to Gillette Castle—the parking area is about .6 mile from the park entrance.

More signs direct you from the parking area to the castle. This eccentric edifice was built between 1914 and 1919 by William Gillette, one of the great figures on the American stage. Acclaimed for his portrayal of Sherlock Holmes, Gillette was born and bred in Connecticut; he lived in the castle until his death in 1937. Unbelievable though it seems, the interior of this building nearly outdoes the exterior. Granite walls, hand-hewn interior oak trim, built-in furniture, intricate wooden locks, and unique light fixtures are only

some of the attractions. The entrance fee to the building, which is open daily from Memorial Day to Columbus Day, is $.50.

After exploring the castle's wonders and perhaps lunching at an adjacent picnic table, walk a few yards to "Grand Central Station," the main terminal for the now-dismantled Seventh Sister Shortline. The three-mile-long miniature railroad was Gillette's pride and joy, and his guests were often treated to a ride while he manned the throttle. The park's trail system crosses, parallels, and follows the old railroad bed. A short piece of track has been preserved near the station.

From the station follow the flagstone ramp down to the sign that reads "Loop Trail to River Vista, 0.5 Mile" and turn left. You wind down through thick young hemlocks interspersed with black birch. Bear left at the first fork. Signs warning people to stay on the trail indicate fragile areas where shortcuts have caused erosion in the past. As you walk, look sharply through the gaps in the trees for some excellent views of the Connecticut River below. After about ¼ mile, the trail circles back along the face of a wall, crosses an attractive footbridge, and rejoins the outward route.

Return to the "Loop Trail" sign and bear left. This pleasant, graded trail passes many mementos of the old railroad. It also takes you past several wooden "dials," innovative methods of explaining natural phenomena along the way. When the arrow on the rotating dial points to an item of interest, a transparent window on the opposite side reveals the corresponding ecological story.

At a four-way trail junction, take the wide path on your left. You are now following the rail-road bed; a few of the old ties still remain in place. Much of the vegetation along this stretch is being choked by the alien Oriental bittersweet.

After passing over a footbridge, the trail curves right. At the fork, go left on the sunken way. Bear right at the circular "7 S RR" sign. Picking up the railroad bed again in a few yards, turn right alongside the tar park entrance road.

The trail appears to end on the road, but in a few yards it heads right, uphill, into the woods again. At the first fork, bear right, and then at the next junction turn left toward the castle. Continue straight downhill; then turn left — you see below you the railroad bed that you started on. At the four-way junction, turn left again. When you reach a large stone cairn, take the right fork across a long footbridge. Now the trail runs along the road that loops around to the parking area. From here you can easily navigate back to your car.

5 Larsen Sanctuary

Total distance: 2½ miles
Hiking time: 1½ hours/Rating: D
Highlights: Nature center, farm pond

Dewberries

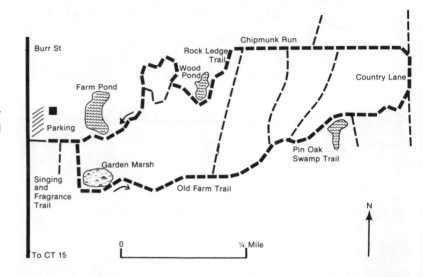

Save this walk for a lazy summer day. An oasis in the urban sprawl of Fairfield County, Larsen Sanctuary is small, and its 6½-mile trail network traverses flat, undemanding terrain. While it lacks the rolling hills and sweeping vistas of many Connecticut trails, intriguing names like Cottontail Cutoff, Dirty Swamp Trail, and Old Farm Trail hint at the diverse habitats it covers. Because of the predominance of low, marshy land so attractive to birds, the sanctuary is a particularly fine birding area.

To reach the sanctuary from the eastbound lanes of the Merritt Parkway (CT 15), take exit 44 in Fairfield and immediately turn right (west). From the westbound lanes, take exit 45, pass under the parkway, and turn right. Either way, you are on Congress Street, which you follow for 1.2 miles to Burr Street. Turn right and drive 1.1 miles to the sanctuary entrance, on the left.

Larsen Sanctuary is owned and run by the Connecticut Audubon Society. The admission fee is $1 for adults and $.50 for unaccompanied children (under 18); there is no charge for Fairfield residents, Connecticut Audubon Society members, or children accompanied by adults.

A massive, modernistic gray building houses the nature center, which, in addition to the usual book store and exhibit areas, has a large auditorium and a library. Both the studious nature lover and the casual browser can spend many a worthwhile hour here.

You approach the trail system through a small structure reminiscent of a covered bridge, located to the right of the center. Pick up a trail map on the way through. From the multitude of paths, we chose a route that hit several points of interest. Although it was early March when we explored the sanctuary, it was alive with birds. A trio of ducks flew overhead and several species sang from the trees and underbrush. We heard the distinctive flutter and owllike moan of the mourning dove and the cheerful (although

far from melodious) cry of that faithful harbinger of spring, the red-winged blackbird.

The trail, at the start strewn with wood chips, heads left through scattered, overgrown apple trees past the Singing and Fragrance Trail for the blind, off to the right. Mountain laurel and rhododendron flank that trail, while a pair of open fences mark the way.

In a few yards, you reach an open, glass-walled stand with seasonally slanted exhibits. At the fork bear right on Old Farm Trail. The trail sign here, as elsewhere in the sanctuary, is posted above arm's reach to discourage vandals. On the right, a massive grapevine twists along a stone wall before arching upwards to cling to the upper branches of a great, old apple tree.

As you pass Garden Marsh

Pond on the left, note the wood duck nesting boxes set on poles above the water. Sweet-scented honeysuckle vines festoon many trees along the marshy pond's edge, and heavy growths of sharp, spiny greenbriar vine guard both sides of the trail.

At the next fork bear right. Shortly you pass a little clearing on the right. Here a trailing vine of the blackberry family, the dewberry, winds around the tall grasses. The rather sour, edible, black berries can be refreshing on a hot, humid day.

Continue on the Old Farm Trail past the Azalea (left), Wildlife (right), and Seep (left) trails to Pin Oak Swamp Trail. Turn to the right here through an opening in a stone wall. Notice how the maple tree on your right has grown over the wire that was once attached to its surface. Deeply buried metal objects such as this have damaged the equipment of many an unsuspecting sawyer!

Proceed past Cottontail Cut-off. The trail now runs the length of a low, earthfill dam. The shallow marshy pond behind it (to your right) is an ideal wildlife habitat.

Bear left at the next two junctions, following Trillium Trail briefly and then Country Lane to Chipmunk Run. Turn sharply left onto this old town road.

You now begin the loop back toward the nature center.

In earlier days, the stone walls on either side separated farmers' fields from passers-by. A short distance past the end of Old Farm Trail (left), the road forks at the top of a small rise. Follow Rock Ledge Trail down the slope to a small brook. Railroad ties set into the hillside provide secure footing here. As you descend look for the unusual, dunce-capped, wood duck nest on the far side of Wood Pond.

The trail crosses the brook below the pond and then forks. The two paths rejoin within a short distance; we chose to continue on Rock Ledge Trail, the right fork. Soon after the left fork comes in, you reach Farm Pond with large numbers of tame mallard ducks and Canada geese — a good place to dispose of leftover bread.

The start of Old Farm Trail, the glass-walled exhibit, and the parking lot are close by. Before leaving the sanctuary, visit the compound for injured animals behind the center. Here, with a special permit from the state, the Connecticut Audubon Society treats more than 500 injured animals each year. Most are eventually returned to the wild.

6 Hurd State Park

Total distance: 2½ miles
Hiking time: 1½ hours/Rating: CD
Highlights: Connecticut River views

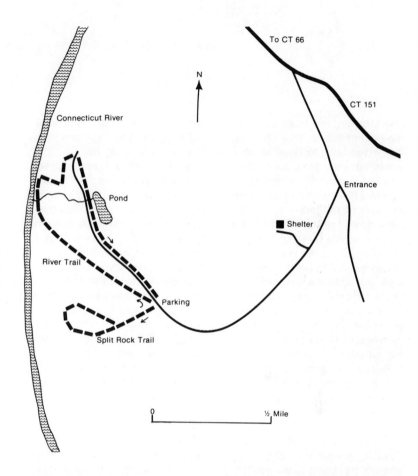

Serendipity. It's a lovely sounding word with a beautiful meaning: "the faculty of making fortunate and unexpected discoveries by accident." Perhaps the most famous example of serendipity was Sir Alexander Fleming's discovery of penicillin while investigating the noxious green mold that was killing his bacteria cultures. For a hiker, serendipity is a familiar byword. In this book we point out what we have seen, but you should always be prepared for serendipitous happenings. Remember that "adventure is not in the guidebook, and beauty is not on the map."

With this thought in mind, pay a visit to secluded Hurd State Park, perched on the east bank of the Connecticut River. From the junction of CT 151 and CT 66 in Cobalt, drive south on CT 151 for 2.4 miles and bear right at the Hurd State Park sign. You reach the park entrance, on the right, in .5 mile. Another right turn .5 mile down this road leads to a delightful, rainy-day picnic shelter with two great stone fireplaces and tables galore. To reach the trails, however, drive past the picnic shelter road to the "Split Rock Trail" sign, 1.1 miles from the park

Tugboat and barge on the Connecticut River

entrance. There is ample parking here.

As we entered the park on a recent hike, we saw a bluebird, the first we'd spotted in a few years. Bluebirds are the same shade as the most breathtaking patch of sky you've ever seen. Unfortunately their numbers have dropped sharply because of competition from two drab aliens — the English sparrow and the starling. A few people are trying to redress the balance by constructing bluebird trails

with a series of just-so bird houses along forest margins. With luck and the effort of dedicated people, this too rare sight will again become common.

Follow Split Rock Trail left onto an old tote road and thence to a well-trodden path. (The River Trail also starts here; save it for later.) Selected trees along the trail are identified with signs, each in the shape of the tree's leaves.

Walking along here early

one morning, we froze at a movement farther down the trail. A spotted fawn tottered to an uncertain stop, eyed us a bit, snorted to absorb our smell better, and—deciding we were dubious characters—bounded back down the trail. Serendipity!

After ¼ mile or so of gentle climbing, leave the trail at the first grassy area on the left and walk out onto a white rock ledge for clear views. Across the river to the left is Bear Hill (see Hike 43). Only power lines —progress—mar this view of the hills along the river.

Bear right on this long, down-hill rock ledge, drinking in the river views as you progress. Watch your step—the rock ledge is neatly split by a narrow crevice, twenty-five feet deep. Shortly, beyond the split, cut sharply right and climb back uphill parallel to the ledge. After passing a great white glacial erratic, rejoin the trail and re-trace your steps to the trail signs.

Now take the River Trail, which proceeds leisurely down-hill through ferns and other undergrowth to a large grassy picnic area beside the river. Across the river to the right you can see the United Tech-nologies jet engine facility. The grassy clearing is a popular camping area for boaters plying the river. In addition to private craft, tugs propelling rusty barges occasionally chug by.

Spend a while exploring the riverside. Wandering off to the left, we saw two young black ducks in a quiet spot. The trees here are different from those on the surrounding hillsides; syca-mores, dying elms, tall sassafras, cottonwoods, silver maples, and willows form this forest canopy. The open areas, covered with coarse grass glistening with dew in the morning, are fringed with bouncing bet and podded milkweeds. Retrace your steps and continue right along the riverbank and across the stream—note the path and two tote roads on the right. After exploring the northern end of the riverside grassy area, head uphill on any one of these three trails; they all join shortly.

There is a hand pump where the three routes meet—you might stop for a drink. Continue steadily uphill keeping the brook ravine on your right. At the next fork bear left and curve slowly right with the trail until you emerge on the tar park road. Turning right, you pass a rock wall built by the Civilian Conservation Corps (CCC) in the 1930s on your right and a frog pond on your left before reaching your car.

7 Highland Springs and Lookout Mountain

Total distance: 2½ miles
Hiking time: 1½ hours/Rating: C
Highlights: Highland Springs, hemlock grove, views

Wood frog

Billed as the "Purest and Best Table Water in the World," bottled mineral water from the two springs at Highland Park was once distributed throughout southern New England and as far away as New Jersey. Although the bottling business, a thriving enterprise during the latter half of the nineteenth century, is now defunct, the two springs are not. Their waters are piped to an outlet near the Highland Springs parking lot for the use of area residents and hikers on the Highland Park Loop of the Shenipsit Trail system. The icy-cold spring water is the perfect complement to this delightful woodland walk—especially on a hot summer day.

The loop trail begins at the Highland Springs parking lot. From US 6 in the center of Manchester, drive south on CT 83 to Spring Street, a left turn .3 miles beyond the I-84 overpass. Follow Spring Street 2.7 miles to Highland Springs.

Before starting out, look for the two large piebald sycamores standing near the trail head. The piebald effect results from the sycamore's normal growth; while the bark of most trees splits into vertical furrows as new wood forms just inside it, the sycamore's bark breaks off in plates, leaving a clean white surface which contrasts markedly with older, darker bark.

From the parking lot, follow the road uphill into a thick stand of hemlocks, keeping the chain-link fence on your left. Light blue blazes crossed with a horizontal yellow stripe mark your way. Turn right off the road at the fork just past the double blaze and then left at the second fork a short distance beyond. The well-worn trail now climbs steadily, and the reassuring blue and yellow blazes appear from time to time with occasional blue arrows where the trail turns.

In about ¾ mile you cross the old cinder road. The hemlock begins to thin out until it is almost wholly replaced with oak and a scattering of maple, hickory, and black birch. The soil here may look the same, but the water-loving roots of the hemlock know the difference.

After another ¼ mile you come to a four-way junction. The blue and yellow blazes go right, but you should continue straight ahead onto the blue-blazed Shenipsit Trail, which leads to Gay City State Park (see Hike 17) some six miles to the south. Today you only follow the blue blazes a short distance past a screen of laurel to a thirty-foot-high hemlock. Look to the right—you see a mysterious clearing where only sedges and mosses grow. Surrounding the opening are numerous high-bush blueberry plants that are heavily laden in season. Unfortunately the berries, although beautiful, are extremely sour —perhaps because of a very acid soil. We don't know why no woody plants grow within the opening; it's possible that the spring snow-melt flooding kills them. But some mysteries should be left that way—the dark corners of life are some of the most precious. In another age this might have been considered a witches' trysting ground!

Retrace your steps to the junction and follow the blue and yellow blazes to the left up a small rise to a gravel clearing, the summit of Lookout Mountain (744 feet). Note carefully where you enter the clearing to ease your way back onto the trail. Benches and picnic tables bid you welcome.

The view from the lookout depends on visibility—too often Connecticut Valley smog reduces your horizon. Manchester lies in the foreground, but because of its well-treed streets, this city of 50,000 is hard to see. Only the flat, smoke-stacked box of the hospital and the white spire of the Center Congregational Church are readily identifiable. In the middle distance the towers and

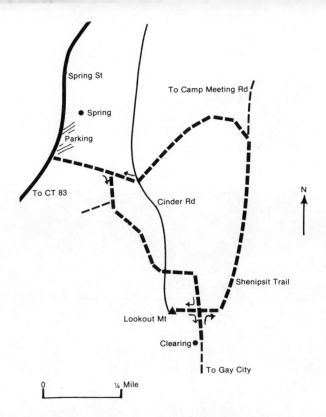

Spring St

● Spring

Parking

To CT 83

To Camp Meeting Rd

Cinder Rd

N

Shenipsit Trail

Lookout Mt

Clearing ●

To Gay City

0   ¼ Mile

high-rise office buildings of Hartford stand out, and on a very clear day you can see the white finger of the Heublein Tower (see Hike 34) rising from Talcott Mountain northwest of Hartford.

Return once again to the junction, and proceed straight across onto the joint Shenipsit Trail/Highland Park Loop. The trail curves gently left along the top of a ridge above an old granite quarry. To the right the land drops off quickly in stepped ledges to a flat forest floor. On the left lies a long narrow depression which snow melt floods each spring. At this time of year it also serves as a breeding ground for the wood frogs.

These black-masked, tan-colored frogs are the earliest spring breeders of our native amphibians. Although probably

more numerous than the familiar spring peepers, they lack the melodious high-pitched cry of the latter and are therefore less familiar. You often hear their low croaks in this area as early as the fourth week in March. The tadpoles must go through their metamorphosis and become small frogs quickly, since the depression is dry by summer.

The thin, poor soil along the exposed ledges of the ridge dries out quickly and is largely treed by chestnut oaks, which are more tolerant of poor, dry soil than the hemlocks. With their deep-furrowed, dark gray bark, these oaks are distinctive at any season. The trail now slopes down to meet the flat forest floor. Hemlocks are thick about the trail again—a legacy of Highland Springs on the other

side of the hill. Watch carefully for a double blaze and an arrow on a large chestnut oak to the left of the trail near the end of the ridge. At the fork, turn left uphill. (The blue-blazed Shenipsit Trail continues straight and crosses Camp Meeting Road in about two miles.)

The blazes, again blue with a horizontal yellow bar, run only a short distance toward the chain-link fence separating town from private properties. Just before reaching the fence, you pass a lightning-riven hemlock. Notice the strip of removed wood and bark slashing down one side of the tree. The extreme temperatures induced by the lightning vaporized the sap of the tree, causing the wood literally to explode.

Although there are no blazes here, continue along the Highland Park Loop keeping the fence on your right. Shortly the fence joins the cinder road you crossed earlier. Continue along the road, bearing left at the fork where the cinder road goes under the fence. After ¼ mile you should reach the blue and yellow-blazed trail which runs with the road you took at the beginning of the hike. Retrace your steps to your car—but pause for a refreshing drink of spring water before leaving!

8 Wadsworth Falls

Total distance: 3 miles
Hiking time: 1¾ hours/Rating: CD
Highlights: Waterfalls

Fishermen at Big Falls

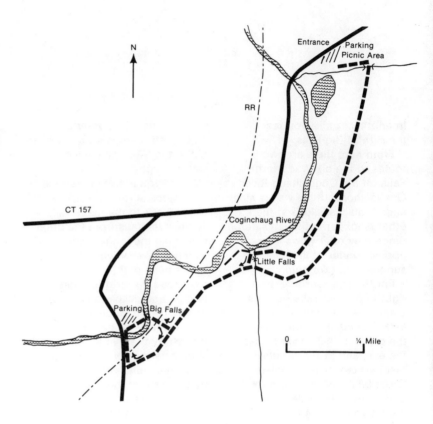

Moving water has a special fascination for man that is rivaled only by the flickering of fire. The ebb and flow of ocean waves mesmerize us, boiling rapids and cascades captivate our attention, and waterfalls enchant us wherever they occur. This hike features not one but two of these attractions. Best viewed during spring's heavy runoff, the larger of this pair is none-theless worth a visit at all seasons.

From the junction of CT 66 and CT 157 in Middletown take CT 157 southwest, following signs to Wadsworth Falls. You reach the park entrance on the left in 1.6 miles. There is a $1 parking fee on summer week-ends. The park features swim-ming, bathhouses, picnic tables, fireplaces, and hiking trails.

A nice, although not totally reliable, carved map of the park's trails has been set up just beyond the entrance. From this spot, go left through the picnic grove to the trail that begins near two great white oaks.

Immediately after crossing a bridge over a small stream that splashes down a series of ledges, the trail forks. Bear right. Cedars, maples, birches, and poplars form the woods backdrop, while sweet ferns, yarrow, blackberries, and a large patch of poison ivy line the path.

A short distance farther on, you come to a second small stream. The bridge over this one is supported by side walls of masonry cloaked in a patina of mosses and lichens. Here the woods are composed of tall, straight hemlocks, oaks, and hickories. Red squirrels shout loudly from safe perches far above the trail. Every so often, paths leave the well-worn main way, inviting exploration.

In ½ mile, when the trail splits, take the right fork toward Little Falls (you return by the left path). Winding through beautifully treed ravines and

slopes, the side trail parallels a small stream that slides over mossy ledges. About ¾ mile from the start you reach Little Falls.

Cross the brook below the falls and climb the steep hill on its right. Be careful, as the com-pacted soil can be slippery when wet. On the hilltop, there is a falls overlook to your left.

When you have finished gazing, return to the side trail, which soon reaches the wide, worn main trail—turn right. Less than ¼ mile from the falls and about 1 mile from the start, railroad tracks and power lines appear below on your right.

In another ¼ mile you reach the sign to Big Falls.

From here there are two routes to the big Wadsworth Falls on the Coginchaug River. One is short but the way is steep and, in places, slippery; the other is longer but much safer. Since they offer views from opposite sides of the river, we suggest you take both.

For the shorter route, turn right at the Big Falls sign. As you cross the railroad tracks, look around. The blue bells of the creeping bellflower please the eye, and in season black raspberries tickle the palate. Great banks of multiflora roses and a few striking deptford pinks attract your attention.

Proceed right on the path along the far side of the tracks. For your first view of Big Falls, bear left down a steep, deeply eroded pitch to the brink of the falls. Now head back up a bit, passing through a small stand of handsome, twisted beeches, and take the higher and safer of two parallel paths above the pool lying at the base of the falls. To reach the pool, bear off to the right and down a steep slope.

From this vantage point, you face the cascading water. Ragged volcanic traprock provides the upper layer of erosion-resistant rock always necessary for the maintenance of a waterfall. To the left there is a great under-cut in the traprock carved by water in ages past.

When you are ready retrace your steps across the railroad tracks back to the main trail. To view the falls from the other side, take the longer, safer route, which is now on your right. Keep to the main path until you reach a tar road, turn right, cross the bridge, and descend into the grassy field by a parking lot. Follow the worn path down to the left by the "No Motorcycles" sign. After crossing the edge of a small field, you come out by the base of the falls. You may have to share this spot with fishermen trying to entice elusive brown trout. A fenced-in overlook to the right provides another view.

Return to the main trail for the route back to your car.

9 Greenwich Audubon Sanctuary

Total distance: 3 miles
Hiking time: 1¾ hours/Rating: C
Highlights: Nature center, bird blinds

Mention Greenwich, and you invoke visions of high-walled estates surrounded by dense city and ribbons of concrete. The urban complex of greater New York engulfed this southwest corner of Connecticut long ago. A visit to the 280-acre Greenwich Audubon Sanctuary is a pleasant surprise; its woodland beauty compares favorably with many wilder, less accessible areas of the state. Rolling hills, large growth hardwoods, swamps, a small river, and a pond provide varied habitats which attract many kinds of birds—including the pale-faced, city-jaded hiker.

To reach the sanctuary, take exit 28 from the Merritt Parkway (CT 15) and turn north onto Round Hill Road. After 1.5 miles, turn left onto John Street. Drive for 1.4 miles to Riverville Road; the Audubon center entrance and parking lot are on your right (admission fee: adults, $1; children, $.50; Audubon Society members, free; hours: 9-5, Tuesday-Sunday.)

In addition to maintaining a network of easy trails, the center operates an excellent book store, an interpretive center with seasonal exhibits, and a variety of natural history programs and demonstrations on weekends. All are well worth

Skunk cabbage leaves and spathe in spring

the nominal charge.

Before you begin walking, pick up a map of the trail system at the center. There are no painted blazes here to guide you, but there are signs at trail junctions.

Starting by a large sign showing the trail system in contrasting colors, follow paved Orchard Road left, downhill, through an old orchard dotted with birdhouses. Note the evenly spaced holes in the bark of the first apple tree on your left. These holes are unmistakably the work of a provident woodpecker with the unglamorous name of yellow-bellied sapsucker. He drills the neat rows one day and returns the next to drink the sap that has welled into them and to feast on insects that have been attracted by the free lunch.

The tar surface ends shortly; follow the rutted dirt road briefly before turning right into the woods on Discovery Trail. You pass an old stone spring house on the right. As you rise from a short dip, look for the particularly large white ash on your left. Most of the sanctuary is clothed in towering, rich bottomland hardwoods—beech, ash, tulip, oak, and maple.

Past a small stream, the trail tends downhill. Level log steps partially embedded in and per-

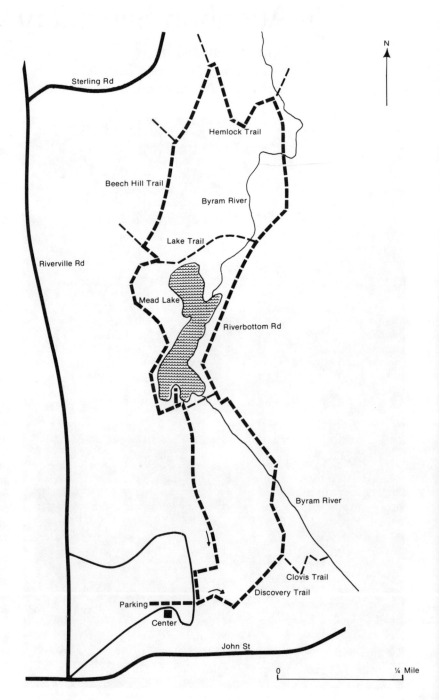

pendicular to the trail here direct water runoff away from the path. Without them, the well-traveled path would rapidly erode. (The wood chips you find elsewhere on the trails are likewise not meant to ease your way but to protect the trail.)

Shortly Clovis Trail leaves on the right. Continue on Discovery Trail to Byram River and then proceed uphill. Clovis Trail returns on the right. Soon Discovery Trail ends. Keep right, uphill, on Riverbottom Road past a thick patch of greenbriar. (The left path goes to Mead Lake.) The stem of this thorny vine is green year round; its tangled masses are particularly distinctive during the leafless months.

The trail now runs atop a low ridge overlooking Mead Lake to your left. Elaborate bird blinds hug the closest shore. You may have noticed a straggly vine clinging to many trees and shrubs along the path. This vine, the Oriental or Asiatic bittersweet, depends entirely on its coiling ability to work skyward, unlike poison ivy and Virginia creeper, which hoist themselves up with the aid of aerial roots. Because the coils cut deep spiral ridges in host plants, often strangling them, bittersweet is considered a pest in the sanctuary.

The trail descends gradually, cutting through a stone wall. Lake Trail leaves on the left to cross Byram River. Proceed straight on Riverbottom Road and bear left at the next junction. You soon reach Byram River again.

The muddy flood plain on the far side is liberally dotted with skunk cabbage, a rather unattractive and malodorous plant that blossoms very early in the spring. Its shape and smell are specially adapted to attract the only insects available for pollination at that time—carrion flies. Attracted by the reddish color of the hoodlike spathe and the fetid odor, the flies mistake skunk cabbage for a dead animal. In the process of investigating it, they pollinate the tiny flowers inside.

After crossing the river, follow the trail up the slope through a large grove of beech trees. Riverbottom Road terminates at the top of this rise. Proceed left, carefully, on Hemlock Trail. This route is not as well worn as most in the sanctuary. Be particularly cautious where the trail zigs sharply right.

This path ends on the crest of another rise. Note the boundary marker—a large pile of small stones resting on a glacial boulder—by the junction. Turn left onto Maple Swamp Trail, which climbs steadily until it meets Beech Hill Trail. Again bear left. This trail drops gradually and merges with Dogwood Lane, which you also follow to the left.

You pass more large beeches. Unfortunately the knife scars on the smooth, tender bark are still quite decipherable.

Soon you reach the west side of Mead Lake. From the trail you can see the bird blinds across the water. The trail leaves the lake and curves left at the base of a hill, where a small bridge spans seasonal streams and wet areas.

Proceed through a stone wall; Lookout Point Trail, a short side track on the left, comes to a dead end at the shore of Lake Mead with a view down its full length. Bear right up Discovery Trail to Orchard Road. Look right for an old root cellar embedded in the hillside before turning left for a short walk back to your car.

10 McLean Game Refuge

Total distance: 3¼ miles
Hiking time: 2 hours/Rating: CD
Highlights: Wildlife, picnic grove

Tucked away in north central Connecticut, the privately endowed McLean Game Refuge was established by George P. McLean, a former governor of Connecticut and U.S. Senator: "I want the game refuge to be a place where trees can grow . . . and animal life can exist unmolested, . . . a place where some of the things God made may be seen by those who love them as I loved them. . . ."

Today, be you hiker or cross-country skier, the refuge's excellent trail network provides access to acres of woodlands teeming with wildlife as McLean had hoped. Although it is hard to predict what you will see on any given hike, a mid-February day witnessed a fairly common, but seldom seen, brown creeper moving in fits and starts up a loose-barked hickory, a flock of bustling chickadees, and a chipmunk breaking his hibernation in the above-freezing temperatures. A small, quick noise proved to be a ruffed grouse taking a few short steps before launching herself with a thunderous roar.

The main entrance to the refuge is located on US 202-CT 10 in Granby, 1 mile south of the junction of US 202 and

In McLean Game Refuge

CT 20. Year-round parking is available by a gate at the end of a short gravel road; unauthorized vehicles are not permitted beyond this point.

An old apple tree stands at the right side of the entrance gate nearly overwhelmed by faster-growing native trees— 'hese living mementos of abandoned farms are scattered throughout Connecticut's woodlands. The unnatural stretching of its upper branches bears witness to its losing battle for life-bearing sunlight. Spring may bring a few delicate blossoms to this aging specimen; fall, tart apples for the deer and hiker.

Walk along the road a short distance to a three-sided shelter on the left. Here is displayed an inviting map of the refuge's interconnecting trails and woods roads. There are three marked loops—blue, yellow, and red —which run together briefly at first. You should concentrate on the blue blazes. Cross the bridge over Bissel Brook just beyond the shelter. The trail starts here on the right.

After ascending a small knoll, look carefully down the slope to the right for two decaying butternut trees. A short-lived member of the walnut family, the butternut tree was used by early settlers as a source of a yellow

water-soluble dye. The nuts have an excellent flavor, but their iron-hard exteriors beneath the sticky green covering are very hard to crack.

The trail, which has been following Bissel Brook, bends away to the left. Where the woods thin out watch carefully on your right for a large dead red pine with a narrow, foot-long, vertical hole in its trunk. Only the jack-hammer bill of the pileated woodpecker can make such an opening. Although the tree is now dead, newer growth around the hole indicates that the cut was made while it was still alive. However, the decayed, honeycombed interior shows that the tree's center had already died and was infested with large carpenter ants—this bird's favorite food. About ¼ mile beyond the tree the red loop trail leaves to the left (distance around red loop: 1¼ miles). You should continue following the blue and yellow blazes.

The trail now tends gently upward. After ½ mile or so, you reach a lovely clearing atop a small rise with the Barndoor Hills peeking through the trees to your right. Shortly, the yellow-blazed trail diverges left (distance around yellow loop: 1¾ miles). Following the blue dots downhill for ¼ mile, you come to a living shagbark hickory on the

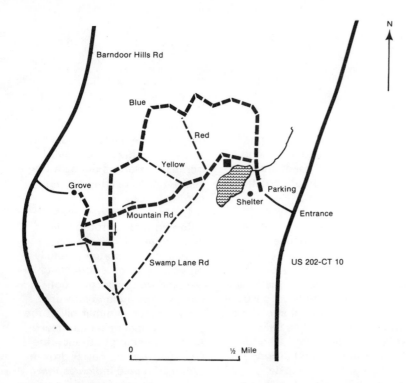

Barndoor Hills Rd

Blue

Red

Yellow

Grove

Mountain Rd

Shelter

Parking

Entrance

Swamp Lane Rd

US 202-CT 10

N

0   ½ Mile

left which has a small wood-pecker hole drilled into its side. A close examination reveals evidence of squirrel habitation—the new growth has been chewed back to permit continued access to the cosy cavity.

Immediately beyond, the trail joins a woods road, and the two together bear left. Watch for a blue arrow on a large hemlock, which signals a right turn through a mixed grove of hemlock and white pine. After a short distance, you cross a gravel road; continue straight on the blue-blazed trail (a left takes you to the parking lot in about 1 mile). Where the trail forks, turn right up a small rise. After ¼ mile, you reach the gravel road again. Here a small triangular

sign, "Footpath to the Grove," beckons—we couldn't resist the invitation. While the blue-blazed trail went left, we went right along the gravel road. The road forks again in ¼ mile; we followed the left branch.

The footpath takes you down a hill to an open hardwood grove with picnic tables, stone fireplaces, and a rustic log cabin which shelters still more picnic tables for the rainy-weather tramper. (This picnic area may also be reached by car from Barndoor Hill Road, a left turn off CT 20, 1 mile west of Granby Center).

After lunch, retrace your steps to the gravel road and turn left to return to the parking area.

You cross the trail you walked up and after ¾ mile pass one of the caretaker cabins, beneath which a raccoon had taken up residence.

Just before you reach your starting point the road skirts a small pond. Be sure to save some bread from your lunch to feed the native fish—since fishing is forbidden, they are quite tame. This is an ideal place for identification! Watch for the flat ovals of sunfish and bluegills, the former distinguished by sharper coloration and a sunburst of yellow on their breasts. The vertical-barred yellow perch, the constantly cruising largemouth black bass (with horizontal side stripes), and swarming shiners complete the list of the pond's bread-feeding fish. Lurking in the weeds, you may see a long, thin pickerel sliding in for a lightning rush to feed on one of the feeders. The pond is also an annual breeding ground for Canada geese. If you look sharply to the right toward the pond's shallow end, you may notice a large brushpile—a beaver lodge. The beavers occasionally create trouble in the refuge by damming up the pond's outlet.

Continue on the road around the outlet end of the pond to your starting point.

11 Pine Knob Loop

Total distance: 2½ miles
Hiking time: 1¾ hours/Rating: B
Highlights: Views

Housatonic Meadows Campground from the North Loop

Located right on the edge of the Housatonic River Valley in western Connecticut, the double peaks of Pine Knob command excellent views of this beautiful river. In contrast to the large and dirty Connecticut River, the Housatonic is a cosy little river winding down a lovely scenic valley—and its upper reaches are still relatively clean. Historic enough to rate a volume in the Rivers of America series, it is currently being studied by the U.S. Bureau of Outdoor Recreation for possible designation as a "Wild and Scenic River."

To reach this hike's start, drive to the western end of Cornwall Bridge (the junction of CT 4 and US 7) and head north on US 7. In 1.1 miles a blue oval sign on the left proclaims "Pine Knob Loop." Although there is a parking area off the road, you may have to compete with trout fishermen for a parking place —the Housatonic is perhaps the premier trout river in the state.

The blue-blazed trail starts on a tote road at the north end of the parking area. Old house foundations and a pleasant crossing of Hatch Brook meet your eye immediately. This section of trail cuts through mixed woods of oak, ash, maple, and

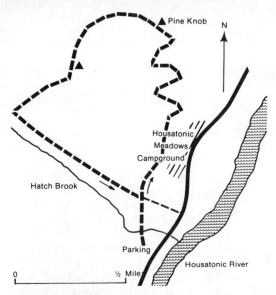

Pine Knob · N · Housatonic Meadows Campground · Hatch Brook · Parking · Housatonic River · 0 · ½ Mile

hickory, with a few crinkly barked black cherry trees scattered throughout. The five-leaved vine climbing many of the pine is Virginia creeper; the leaves of this harmless plant turn flaming crimson in the fall.

In just under ¼ mile, you reach a junction. Continue straight on the North Loop, paralleling the road off to your right. You come to a second junction within ¼ mile; here fork left. (The right fork leads to the campground at Housatonic Meadows State Park.) As you ascend the steep hill, stubby oaks come to predominate on the thin soil between ledge outcroppings.

Where the trail levels a bit, several chestnut saplings grow, awaiting the touch of the deadly blight. This tree was once among North America's most important hardwoods, with nuts that were eagerly sought by both man and beast and extremely durable wood—trunks dead for sixty years remain solid and some are still standing. The

loss of the chestnut was one of our greatest natural calamities. First noticed in New York's Botanical Garden in 1904, the bark-girdling fungus spread quickly, almost eliminating the tree. The chestnut's ability to sprout from roots has kept it as a common small tree; some occasionally even manage to produce a few nuts before the fungus strikes.

In ¼ mile, the state campground and surrounding hills are visible from a rocky outlook. Circling left, the trail starts its final ascent of the first knob over displaced, tumbled ledges. After ¼ mile, the trail continues left along a rocky terrace. As you face the river, the other peak of Pine Knob is visible on the extreme right. On the left, beyond the river, you can see Mohawk Mountain's distinctive tower against the horizon (see Hike 37).

A few years ago while hiking here in the rain with Robert Redington, who laid out Pine Knob Loop, we met an Appa-

lachian Trail "through hiker." This driven breed of hiker feels the need to hike all 2,025 miles of the AT in a single season. The man we met, who had started in Georgia, was moved to distraction by all the road walking he had endured in New York; he was wandering over these ridges, far from the AT, to avoid Connecticut's road sections.

The trail turns right off the overlook and passes over the top of the wooded, viewless first knob (1,120 feet) before dropping down steeply to the col between the two peaks. In another ¾ mile, on the far side of the second knob (1,160 feet), you reach another lookout. Stop and relax—perhaps you'll see a pair of red-tailed hawks gracefully circling the valley as we did.

Continuing off this knob, the trail drops steeply while the sound of unseen flowing water gradually invades your subconscious. In a small hemlock grove ¼ mile from the lookout, watch for a blue arrow directing you sharply left. The depression of Hatch Brook is visible on your right between two large glacial erratics. In another ½ mile, you reach the loop junction you encountered on the way in. Your car is parked less than ¼ mile to your right.

12 Rocky Neck

Total distance: 4 miles
Hiking time: 2 hours/Rating: D
Highlights: Ocean views, sandy beach, state park

Four Mile River and the fogbound bay

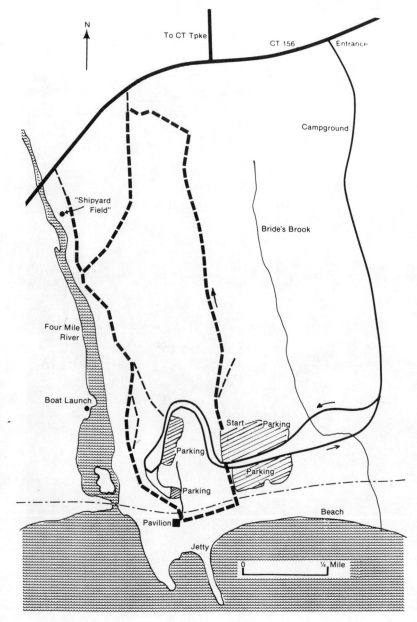

Families sometimes have difficulty finding a place that everyone will enjoy. The outdoor activities at Rocky Neck State Park are varied enough to provide something for everybody. Youngsters can fish off the jetty, teenagers can loll on the beach, and hikers can explore the practically deserted woodland paths.

The park entrance is located off CT 156, 2.7 miles west of CT 161 in Niantic. If you're traveling on the Connecticut Turnpike (I-95), take exit 72 (Rocky Neck) to CT 156 and follow the signs east (left) to the park. In addition to complete day-use facilities—beach, bathhouses, rest rooms, and picnic areas—the park has a separate camping area. The attractive grassy sites set amidst scattered trees may be reserved in advance. In summer, the day-use entrance fee is $1 per car.

Drive into the first large parking area on the right, 1.6 miles from the entrance (where a park map is available) and just beyond Bride's Brook. Head for the far left corner and the picnic tables; the unmarked trail starts to the right of the outhouses. The trail passes quickly through a fringe of oaks and maples to a short causeway leading across a marsh. After walking the causeway just a few yards you are threatened by poison ivy, treated to the sight of large pink swamp roses, startled by ducks you have inadvertently flushed, and delighted by gracefully circling terns.

As you enter the woods beyond the marsh, mountain laurel, sweet pepperbush, blueberries, huckleberries, greenbriar, and sassafras make up the bulk of the undergrowth. Several chestnuts up to thirty feet high are still free of the blight that has ravaged our chestnuts since the beginning of the century. The blight's first sign will be small orange fungal bodies on the bark that indicate the girdling of the trees—a sure sign that they'll be dead soon. Occasional glacial erratics and rounded ledges complete the scene.

At the junction 1½ miles from the start take a short detour right before continuing. The detour leads to a field where Japanese honeysuckle with their highly perfumed yellow and white blossoms grow along the edge.

Retracing your steps and turning left, you arrive at another junction in ½ mile. Turn right; in ¼ mile you reach a woods-locked clearing identified on the park map as Shipyard Field. If you cut through the woods, you emerge on the shore of brackish Four Mile River. A boatyard, a reminder of this hike's shore location, lies across the way. Retrace your steps to the trail junction and go right.

Bear right at the next two forks, finally ascending a rocky ridge. Follow the ridge left toward the ocean. Views, partially obscured at first by oak foliage, then fully open, await you: Four Mile River and the open bay. Clamshells litter the ledges. Gulls drop the clams from on high and then pick out the meat from the shattered shells.

At the end of the open ridge the trail drops down to the left to meet a path. A right turn soon takes you to a tar road. Proceed to the right through a small parking lot to the paved uphill walkway. This leads you beyond the arched bridge over railroad tracks to an imposing pavilion. A make-work project of the 1930s, the pavilion has given full value. The walls of this massive building are made of fieldstone, and large fireplaces cheer the inside. The internal woodwork includes pillars of great tree trunks; at least one was taken from each then-existing state park.

From the front porch of the pavilion curve left toward a picnic area. A rocky fishing jetty thrusts into the water before you, and beyond it spreads the graceful curve of the beach. The rocky arms at either side of the bay provide shelter from all but the roughest storms.

Turn left through the railroad underpass at the near corner of the beach. Swamp roses adorn the embankment here. If you follow the road straight past the concession stands, you will find your car in the second parking lot on the right.

13 Bluff Point

Total distance: 4½ miles
Hiking time: 2¼ hours/Rating: D
Highlights: Beach, ocean views

A combination of historical circumstance and heavy demand for seashore property has kept most of Connecticut's short coastline inaccessible to the general public. Of the very few state parks on the shore, the 778-acre, undeveloped Bluff Point State Park is a special place for the walker. The only such sizable acreage on the Connecticut coast, Bluff Point is free from concessions, cottages, picnic tables, and campsites.

There are no signs to direct you to Bluff Point. From the intersection of CT 117 and US 1 in Groton, drive west for .3 mile on US 1 to Depot Street. Turn left, following this street past Industrial Road and under the railroad tracks (where the paved surface ends) until you reach a gate. You know you have arrived when you spy a sign posting park regulations.

Proceed on foot down the gated dirt road. Fishing boats ply the bay to your right, and windrows of dead eelgrass, one of the few flowering plants that grow in saltwater, line the rocky shore. The brant, a close relative of the Canada goose, feeds almost exclusively on this plant. When a mysterious blight in the 1930s all but exterminated eelgrass, the

Beach flora

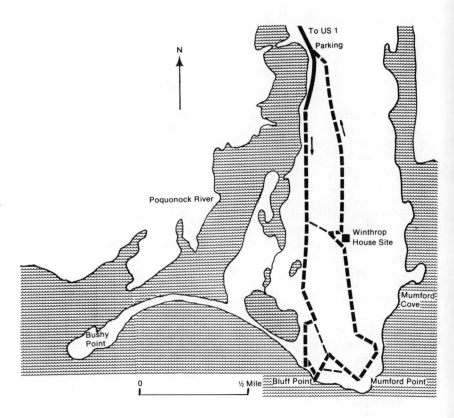

brant nearly went, too. The emaciated flocks subsisted on a diet of sea lettuce until the grass came back. If you walk this way in the colder months, you may see some of the few hundred that winter along the shores of Long Island Sound.

Numerous side paths cut off from the main road. Due to the all-pervading influence of the sea, the woods of Bluff Point are more varied than most inland forests. The tangle of vines and brambles — grape, red-fruited barberry, rose, blackberry, honeysuckle, Oriental bittersweet, and greenbrier — is thick

enough to make any Br'er Rabbit feel at home. Various oaks, cherries, long-thorned hawthornes, tight-barked hickories, shagbark hickories, sumacs, and blueberries represent the deciduous trees and an occasional cedar, the evergreens.

The most common tree in the narrow strip of woods between the road and the bay is sassafras, usually recognized by its mitten-shaped leaves and green-barked twigs. Sassafras leaves actually come in three shapes — like a mitten with no thumb, one thumb, or two thumbs — often on the same branch. Bark peeled from the roots makes a strong tea, which, according to old herbal folklore, purifies the body.

About 1½ miles from your start, you reach the bluffs on the point of land. Over the water to your right lies Groton Heights and to your left, Groton Long Point. Fisher's Island, part of New York, lies to the right of center; Watch Hill in Rhode Island, left of center.

Wander down the ½-mile-long sand spit to Bushy Point on your right. Castoff treasures from the sea await your curiosity: rope; great blocks of wood; blue mussel shells; great whorled whelk shells; marble-sized periwinkle shells; scallop shells; long razor clams; wide, flat strands of kelp; bladder-floated algaes (seaweed); crab husks; and the everlasting, ever-present plastics.

When you've reached the end, turn around and follow the sprawling masses of delicate-looking beach peas back to the bluff. But before you start around the point, pause for a moment among the wild primroses and beach plums. You are standing on a terminal moraine. This hasty-pudding mix of rocks and sand was dumped here some ten thousand years ago when the glacier covering present-day New England retreated.

Follow the road around to the east. Soon after leaving the shore, take the better-worn path left; at the fork 50 yards farther on, bear right. (The trail to the left connects with the outward bound leg of your hike.) Rounding the point, you look over a cattail swamp and stands of tall phragmite reeds, their silky plumes standing sentinel by the sound. Across the bay, a seemingly solid wall of cottages stands in stark contrast to this wild oasis.

The trail moves inland to follow the center ridge of the peninsula. Stone walls stand as mute evidence of colonial cultivation. The trail forks after about ½ mile. This is the site of the Winthrop house. Built around 1700 by Governor Fitz-John Winthrop, grandson of the famous Massachusetts Bay governor, it had a three hundred foot tunnel to the barn and a room-sized brick chimney in the basement for protection from Indian raids.

Leaving the site, take the right fork. (The left joins the bayside road you followed earlier). The path tends left until it joins the outbound trail near the parking lot.

14 Chatfield Hollow

Total distance: 4½ miles
Hiking time: 2¾ hours/Rating: C
Highlights: Views, swimming

Hikers complain about the overuse of a few select areas, yet Connecticut's trails are for the most part underused. As elsewhere, the Appalachian Trail is heavily travelled while most other trails are deserted. If you feel that one of the joys of hiking is leaving the clamor of fellow human beings temporarily behind, consider Chatfield Hollow State Park. Despite several hundred carloads of people in the park on one recent visit here, we met only two youngsters and a group from the New Haven Hiking Club on the well-maintained trails.

Chatfield Hollow lies within that wide band of woodland separating the overdeveloped shore from the inland tier of cities. From the junction of CT 80 and CT 81 in Killingsworth, drive west 1 mile on CT 80. The park entrance is on your right.

Follow the tar road around Schreeder Pond to the parking area on the far side of Oak Lodge Shelter. The pond, which offers fishing, swimming, and picnicking, is the focus of park activity. Walk along the tar road, away from the pond, for a short distance and turn right on the orange-blazed Deep Woods Trail.

The trail moves up a rocky slope along ledges lined with

Waterwheel at Chatfield Hollow

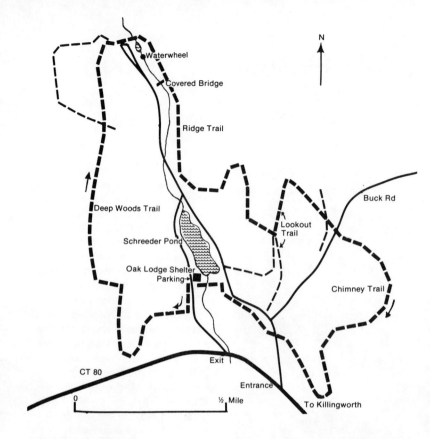

Waterwheel

Covered Bridge

Ridge Trail

N

Buck Rd

Deep Woods Trail

Lookout
Trail

Schreeder Pond

Oak Lodge Shelter
Parking

Chimney Trail

Exit

CT 80

Entrance

0   ½ Mile

To Killingworth

laurel. In ½ mile, the path curves
right off the ledges, then passes
beneath them. The rock face is
stained with mosses and lichens,
and trees sprout from great
cracks. Above you, large red
cedars take advantage of the
bare, flat ledges.

Near a small brook crossing,
a park naturalist has attached
signs to many trees—among
them white cedar, yellow birch,
black birch, witch hazel, chestnut, white oak, red oak, sassafras, tulip, blue beech, American
beech, pignut hickory, white ash,
and flowering dogwood. The
least common in Connecticut
of those identified are two specimens of tupelo, or black gum.

After passing a blue-blazed trail

twice, the 1½-mile orange trail
finally ends at the tar park road.
After enjoying a refreshing drink
from the hand pump, proceed left
across the bridge and around the
dammed-up pool to pick up the
red-blazed Ridge Trail. Initially,
this footpath parallels a stream
that passes a covered bridge and
an undershot waterwheel (the
water flows beneath the wheel
rather than over it). It then
curves left uphill through pines.
In ¾ mile, you come within yards
of the central park road before
turning back uphill.

In another ¼ mile you reach
a T junction. Both paths are well
worn; take the unmarked left. Be
careful at the T; if you miss this
turn, you'll emerge on the park

road across the pond from your
car. You should reach the white-
blazed Lookout Trail in about
50 yards; again bear left.

The white-blazed trail continues to open ledges with a
good southern view through the
hollow. Foster Lake is visible
on the far side of CT 80. From
this vantage point, the trail
curves down, meeting green-
blazed Chimney Trail and a
second blue-blazed trail. Follow
the green blazes across gravel
Buck Road. You cross a boulder-
choked stream twice and follow
its downstream course before
moving away to the left. Ridges
raised by moles burrowing beneath the trail are common here.

As you curve right downhill,
you clamber over and then parallel a stone wall. The trail bends
right again around a mass of
ledges and cleft rocks. These
mammoth chunks form several
caves; the trail drops down
through the largest—the so-
called Indian Cave.

Below the caves, a plank
bridges a swampy brook. As you
walk across, notice the wakes
moving down the long, shallow
pool at left—native brook trout.
Soon you pass through a large,
level stand of red pine adorned
with poison ivy.

When you reach the tar road,
bear right. Your car is parked
½ mile along the road.

15 White Memorial Foundation

Total distance: 5 miles
Hiking time: 2¾ hours/Rating: D
Highlights: Nature center, swamp boardwalk

The 4,000-acre White Memorial Foundation wildlife sanctuary in Litchfield was established in the true spirit of multiple use. Within its boundaries lie over thirty miles of crisscrossing trails (including one for the blind), a family campground, a marina, a retail lumber outlet, and the Litchfield Nature Center and Museum. To balance the more unusual sanctuary uses, 200 acres have been set aside in four untouched natural preserves. These areas provide bases against which environmental changes in adjacent tracts can be judged. The easy 5-mile hike described here explores only a small part of this special sanctuary.

Follow US 202 west 2.2 miles past the junction of CT 118 in Litchfield, and turn left by the signs for the foundation. The gravel entrance road leads .5 mile to a parking area near the large white house that is home to the nature museum (open from 9 A.M. to 5 P.M., Tuesday through Saturday, and from 2 P.M. to 5 P.M., Sunday; admission free but donations welcome).

A rewarding half-hour can be spent looking over the museum's attractive wildlife, geology, and Indian artifact

Stepping stones across the swamp

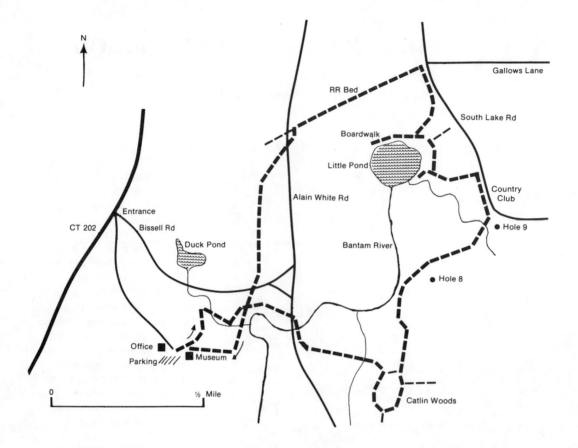

N

RR Bed

Gallows Lane

Boardwalk

South Lake Rd

Little Pond

Alain White Rd

Country Club

● Hole 9

Entrance

Bissell Rd

Bantam River

CT 202

Duck Pond

● Hole 8

Office

Parking ///// ■ Museum

0   ½ Mile

Catlin Woods

exhibits. A book shop specializing in natural history sells pamphlets and maps relevant to the area. Since the numerous trails through the foundation's land twist, turn, and cross each other with wild abandon, a map is a good investment.

We laid out a somewhat intricate route that pleased our impulses. If you lose your way, however, it's easy enough to take alternate trails or roads back to the museum.

To reach the blue-blazed Mattatuck Trail our hike follows for much of the way, bear left across the open field opposite

the museum to the roped end of the self-guiding trail for the handicapped. Soon after passing a large stand of sighing pines, the roped trail bears left. Follow the blue blazes straight through a forest of hemlocks, oaks, and large yellow birches. Curving right, the trail enters a swamp dotted in early spring with yellow marsh marigolds to join a red-blazed trail. Square stepping stones and small log bridges ease your way.

The path proceeds through a thick stand of young white pine to a hard dirt road. Turn left onto the road, walk a short dis-

tance, and then turn right on the blue-blazed Mattatuck. This trail roughly parallels Bantam River. Watch for hobblebushes, which have flat-topped flower clusters and opposite circular leaves. This member of the viburnum family, although more common further north, paradoxically seems to bloom more profusely in Connecticut. The showy, sterile, outer flowers encircle tiny inner ones that eventually turn to coral red drupes.

When you reach paved Alain White Road, cross the river on an abandoned bridge and follow the blue blazes left to gated

Catlin Road. You pass masses of shadbush as you enter Catlin Woods, one of the four natural areas in the sanctuary.

By Miry Brook, the gray patina of old cut stumps tells of former beaver activity. At the first woods road to the right, leave the blue-blazed trail for a short jaunt through this preserve of white pines, hemlocks, and transition hardwoods. In less than ¼ mile and within sight of a gravel road ahead, turn sharply left onto another woods road. The numerous log barriers you see may have been placed here to thwart the ubiquitous trail bike but more probably are jumps for the horse taffic.

Upon reaching the blue-blazed Mattatuck Trail again, bear left. Shortly the blazes bear off to the left; proceed right along the woods road, a causeway through the swamp. Tiny, floating leaves of duckweed turn the still waters into a thin, green carpet.

With the Bantam River to your left, you emerge on the green of a golf course—hole eight of the Litchfield Country Club. The fading woods road bends slowly left across the green, crosses the river, and leads to the right uphill past hole nine. Bear left onto a dirt road past more greens and left again at the fork. The road continues to the edge of the woods, where a great log marked with a red triangle makes a perfect spot for lunch—or just museful sitting.

Now head left towards Bantam River, turn right at the first fork, and then right again at the next junction by the river bank. You eventually reach the point of land between the river and Little Pond. The large sandbar off the river's mouth marks where the slowing current dumps its load of silt.

Retrace your footsteps, taking your first left. Continue to bear left at the next three forks as you curve around the pond. Planks bridging a small stream lined with wild iris lead to an open swamp. A boardwalk, the product of two summers' work by a dedicated individual, enables you to inspect the swamp's mysteries without getting your feet wet. If the boardwalk is still as rickety as it was when we last passed through, skip it.

Return to the footpath and turn left just before the bridge. This path leads to the dirt extention of South Lake Road. A left turn takes you to Gallows Lane and an abandoned railroad bed. Proceed left down the latter, past a cemetery and colony of lazy beavers (they use the railroad bed for their main dam with only a few damlets to shore up low spots) to Alain White Road.

Head across the pavement and bear left on a woods road, crossing a plank bridge. As you enter the pine forest, bear left onto the red-blazed trail. Upon reaching the blue-blazed Mattatuck, continue straight, following the blue dots past paved Bissell Road to the hard dirt road you walked earlier. Rather than retrace your steps through the swamp, continue straight across the bridge over Bantam River. The paved road to the right takes you back to the parking lot.

16 Penwood

Total distance: 4.6 miles
Hiking time: 2½ hours/Rating: C
Highlights: Good views, ridge-top pond

Lady-slippers

The volcanic ridges flanking the Connecticut Valley offer secluded hiking on the outskirts of the central cities. Penwood State Park sits atop one such ridge. Only a few minutes drive from the city, the trails of Penwood carry you beyond the sights and sounds of our workaday world to a place where the most blatant intrusions are the blue blazes marking your way on the Metacomet Trail.

The park entrance is on the north side of CT 185, 1 mile west of the CT 185-CT 178 junction in Bloomfield. There is enough space for a few cars to park on the left just inside the entrance. After the hike, you may want to drive slowly around the circular loop through the park.

Pick up the blue blazes of the Metacomet and follow them a short distance down the right-hand road. Just past a barred tote road bear left into the woods, climbing quickly onto the hemlock-shrouded traprock ridge. Once on top, the trail undulates gently within the forest, which dampens out the sights and sounds of our harried world. Even the park road is invisible. Here the thick woods limit the undergrowth to a few striped maples, wild sarsaparilla, and mapleleaf viburnum.

In 1.8 miles, the trail crosses the far end of the loop road. Take a break from the hike to explore the little ridge-top pond. Head left across the pavement onto a short boardwalk leading through the swamp to the edge of the pond. The teeming fecundity of life here makes the dry forested ridges look like a desert.

Discounting the usual forest birds that are drawn to this cornucopia, we saw or heard more varieties of living things in just a few minutes standing by the pond than in the total time spent on the ridge: dragonflies with outstretched wings, damselflies with folded wings, waterstriders miraculously traversing the surface, circling whirligig beetles setting a dizzying pace when disturbed, and water boatmen riding just under the water's surface. Gayly colored butterflies sat in marked contrast to their mud perches absorbing moisture from their surroundings. Tadpoles were visible along the pond's edges as they came up for an occasional gulp of air. Through the water flicked aquatic newts, the adult form of the red efts found on the forest floor after a spring night of gentle rain. Here and there small frogs popped up, still exhibiting the rounded softness of the recent tadpole stage. And two small water snakes were

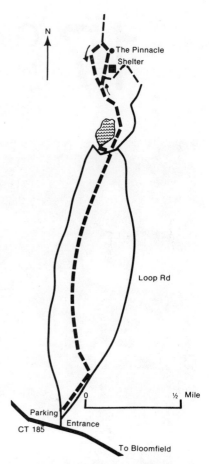

sunning themselves beside the boardwalk.

Even the vegetation here is varied and lush. Lily pads dot the surface. Marsh fern, swamp loosestrife, and buttonbush edge the pond, and a sour gum tree grows on your right. The white blossoms of swamp azaleas perfume the air. Look for the few clumps of swamp juneberry amidst the alders. Their lustrous black berries, which resemble large huckleberries, make a nice snack. If such a place fascinates you as it does us, read the book *Watchers at the Pond* by Francis Russell.

When ready, return to the loop road and continue with the blue blazes left past the large butternut tree. At the double blaze, turn right uphill. Here the steep slope is eased by a long flight of traprock steps. You emerge at the top by a magnificent sealed-off cabin.

Continue following the blazes left to a fine scenic lookout called the Pinnacle. The ridge traversed by the Tunxis Trail lies straight across the valley. On the left rises Heublein Tower (see Hike 34) and farther left, the great tilted volcanic slabs of Mount Higby (see Hike 33).

The blue-blazed trail moves down the far side of the prominence and along the ridge. In a few hundred yards, the trail

cuts left downhill on an old scree slope. Scree, which is loose broken rock weathered off rock masses, tends to migrate almost imperceptibly downhill. Here tree root systems have largely solidified the slope, but in so doing the trees themselves have acquired a bow, offering mute testimony to the power of weather and gravity.

When you reach the base of the hill, follow the blue blazes left along the flat, back to the end of the tar loop road. Retrace your steps back over the ridge's central spine to your car.

17 Gay City

Total distance: 5 miles
Hiking time: 2¾ hours/Rating: CD
Highlights: Abandoned town, state park

Gay City was founded in 1796 by a religious group led by Elijah Andrus. Andrus left for reasons unknown, and in 1800 John Gay, for whom the settlement was named, was appointed president of the remaining twenty-five families. Even for those strict times they were an unsociable group; an itinerant peddler was robbed, murdered, and thrown into a town charcoal pit, and a blacksmith's assistant was slain by his employer for failing to show up for work.

The two most prominent families were the Gays and the Sumners, whose rivalry outlasted the town. Gays called it Gay City and Sumners called it Sumner, although it seems the settlement was known locally as Factory Hollow. To further confuse the issue, when the Foster sisters, descendants of the Sumners, deeded the 2,000-acre area to the state in the 1940s, they stipulated that it be called Gay City!

The town's decline, well underway before the Civil War, followed the usual pattern of hardscrabble areas; the old died and the young left. A paper mill outlasted all the houses; when it burned in 1879 the town was gone. Join us in a hike along the empty dirt roads of this New

Site of the mill wheel

England ghost town.

Gay City State Park is located off CT 85 just south of the Bolton-Hebron town line. In addition to the ten numbered hiking trails, the park offers swimming and picnicking; facilities include outhouses, bathhouses, picnic tables, outdoor fireplaces, and, in the summer, a refreshment stand. There is a $1 fee for parking inside the park gates on summer weekends.

In emulation of thrifty Yankees our hike avoids the toll by parking just outside the gates on the right off the entrance road, where there is room for a few cars. Walking in on the paved road you pick up a few features you might otherwise miss. Fields separated by stone walls grace both sides, and picnic tables are scattered throughout the area.

You soon pass an old graveyard on the right—save it for your return. There are occasional blue blazes on the trees. Continue on the paved road to the North Trail, Trail 2, a blue-blazed tote road ¼ mile from the entrance. Follow this trail straight. Just beyond Trail 10 on the left, turn right onto the Pond Loop. The loop path soon merges briefly with a utility line before forking left on an old tote road. This woods road reaches the parking lot in about ¼ mile. Cross the lot, passing a brown,

painted notice board, and continue downhill on a non-vehicular gravel road to the beach area along the pond, which boasts a small island dotted with evergreens in its center.

Bear left along the edge of the pond to the dam, continuing past Trail 6, which leads to an attractive footbridge across the dam on the right. Bear left as the trail runs along the top of a small earthen ridge. The ridge formed a small canal that diverted water from the pond to power the old paper mill downstream. The pond and the canal assured an even flow; the system damped out high water and accumulated water for controlled periods of operation during droughts.

In just under ¼ mile the trail drops to the right off the canal bank and crosses a bridge over the mill's waterwheel sluiceway. On the left are the squared blocks of the building's foundation and the square hole that diverted flow from the canal to the sluiceway. The canal was reputed to be ten feet deep in its heyday.

Follow the path along Blackledge River to the bridge and cross over. Here the trail forks. Bear right on the North Trail, the old Gay City Road that was the main route to Glastonbury and the Connecticut River. (Left-

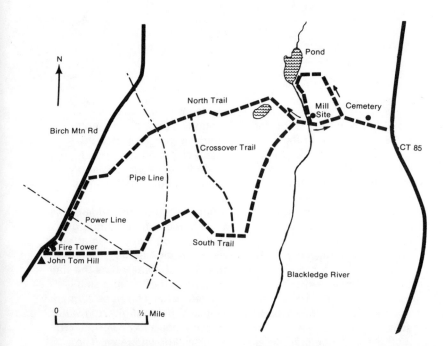

N

Birch Mtn Rd

North Trail

Pond

Mill Site

Cemetery

CT 85

Crossover Trail

Pipe Line

Power Line

Fire Tower
▲ John Tom Hill

South Trail

Blackledge River

0   ½ Mile

branching South Trail, Trail 3, is your return route.)

Along this section in the spring you may hear the drumming of the male ruffed grouse. He finds a good log to give his wings some freedom and then beats them faster and faster until they become a blur. The resulting low-pitched thumping supposedly attracts females and warns away other males. The first time you hear this sound you may think it's a distant motor running or wonder if you are really hearing something. It is a very low-pitched sound—a soft buffeting of the ears. In fact, it is the heartbeat of the New England woods!

The old road climbs gradually. Alert ears will hear occasional noises from the brush: the dash and chirp of the chipmunk,

the heavy-bodied bouncing of the gray squirrel, the scratch-chewink of the towhee, a common woodland bird with a black back, rufous sides, and a white belly.

In just under 1 mile North Trail crosses the Algonquin Gas transmission line, which is heavily used by trail bikes as evinced by the eroded path down its center. Soon climbing more steeply, the trail goes through a patch of laurel and enters an orchard in about ½ mile. Follow the orchard edge to Birch Mountain Road and bear left. Atop the hill, just past the fire tower ½ mile from the orchard, you enter the woods on the left on the South Trail.

The South Trail is a lovely footpath which descends grad-

ually to the power line swath. Proceed to the right here for about 20 feet before crossing the line and reentering the woods. About ½ mile from Birch Mountain Road the trail crosses a brook and soon traverses the same gas pipeline you encountered on the North Trail. In another ½ mile, the trail joins and bears right on a tote road. Continue to the fork with the North Trail (in about ¾ mile). Just before this fork note the old cellar hole to your left; it is one of many in the park.

Retrace your steps over the river and bear right, bypassing the paper mill foundation. Continue bearing slightly right uphill on the blue-blazed tote road. You pass another old cellar hole on your right fronted by four massive, decaying sugar maples. Continue back to the tar road toward your car.

Stop now at the graveyard. It tells a poignant story of the dour little settlement. It's a small plot—a mere dumping ground for the dead. The rival Gays and Sumners are planted on opposite ends of the cemetery. The outlook and character of this vanished town may be reflected in the harsh epitaph on a seven-year-old girl's grave:

"Com pritty youth and see The place where you will shortly be."

18 Soapstone Mountain

Total distance: 4.2 miles
Hiking time: 2½ hours/Rating: C
Highlights: Upland woods, limited views

Soapstone—an intriguing name for a mountain—sits in the 6,000-acre Shenipsit State Forest. A quarry on the east slope used by Indians and early settlers once yielded the soft, talclike, greasy, lustered stone from which the mountain derives its name. In colonial times, the stone was valued for its high heat retention; flannel-wrapped hot soapstones lessened the shock of icy bedclothes.

Soapstone Mountain is located east of the Connecticut River in Somers. From the junction of CT 140 and CT 83, drive north on CT 83 for 3.9 miles to Parker Road and turn right. After 1.3 miles (the last .4 mile is a rough, three-season dirt road), turn right again onto Soapstone Road. There is limited parking on the left in .4 mile where the blue-blazed Shenipsit Trail crosses the road.

Follow the trail to the right. (The way left leads to the beginning of the northern section of the Shenipsit about three miles south.) The forest you will hike through has a lovely, soothing monotony. An understory of maples and black birches struggles for sunlight in the gaps between large red oaks. The leaf-littered floor is carpeted with

Small pond along the Shenipsit Trail

masses of ground pine and wild lily-of-the-valley. Many of Connecticut's hardwood forests are, like this one, all of a size. The last great cutovers were in the early years of this century, and since then cutting has been sporadic — far less than the annual growth.

Not long after leaving Soapstone Road, you reach the first of many trail junctions. At this one, bear right. Watch your turns as there are many paths and old tote roads in this area. If you're woolgathering, it is very easy to lose your way and find that the worn path you're traveling is devoid of blue blazes; in that event retrace your steps to the last blaze and try again.

Shortly you come to a beautiful pile of dirt, possibly the residue left from some early digging or the earth ball from a completely rotted, wind-thrown tree. The pile is almost unrecognizable, so encrusted is it with mosses, algae, and lichens in lovely shades of green and almost iridescent grays. A few sprouting birches point to the pile's eventual demise.

The fairly smooth path steepens, becomes rockier, climbs a small rocky defile, and curves right. About .2 mile from the start, you have a partial view south when the leaves are off the trees. However, this

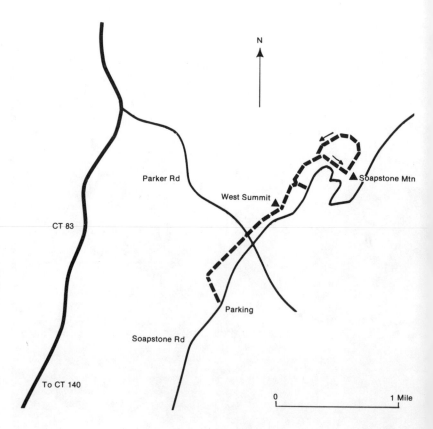

and similar views grow dimmer with continued forest growth.

We passed through here once at a magic time of year—the small leaflets bursting their buds had spread a delicate, light green blush over the forested hills. A week earlier and the hills would still have had a stark wintry look; a week later and inexorable growth would have clothed all. This is the easiest season to miss—the brief, precious moment of transition.

At .7 mile, you cross Parker Road and shortly bear left. The swamp at left is happy in spring, echoing with the high-pitched chorus of spring peepers. We have all heard countless thousands of these tiny tree frogs, but have you ever seen one? Cautious creeping in the evening with a flashlight may reward you with the sight of one of these tan frogs, whose throat swells into a great white bubble-like soundbox from a body less than one inch long. Summer sightings are more a matter of quick eyes, quicker hands, and luck. Most of the woodland hoppers you find are black-masked wood frogs, but occasionally you find one without the mask and a faint contrasting "X" on his back—this is the spring peeper!

The trail ascends another rocky outcropping over upward-tipped ledges. Laid down in flat layers millions of years ago, these protruding ledges were tilted by subsequent crustal deformations.

In spring fern fiddleheads pop up everywhere. Instead of growing gradually like most annuals, the fern unrolls like a New Year's Eve favor from a tightly curled mass into a fully grown plant. In northern New England the fiddleheads of the ostrich fern are considered a delicacy.

The trail has been rolling slowly upward and after 1.1 miles reaches the rocky west summit of Soapstone Mountain (930 feet). Near the top you find an atypical species of violet: the northern downy violet. The leaves are oval and fuzzy rather than heart-shaped and smooth, but the familiar violet blue flowers are unmistakable.

On a leafless day the microwave tower on Soapstone Mountain proper appears across the small valley. The trail works downhill and near the bottom is steep and badly eroded by trail bikes. You pass quite near Soapstone Road on the right before joining a tote road that leads you left downhill. The blue trail leaves the road .5 mile from the west summit and heads to the right up Soapstone Mountain—a good steady climb. (The yellow blazes on the tote road bypass the summit and rejoin the blue trail in .4 mile.) Climbing, you reach the top (1,075 feet) 1.9 miles from your start. Note the geodetic survey marker set in a boulder with SOAPSTONE engraved across it.

There used to be an old fire tower here with a 360-degree view, but it has recently been replaced with a privately owned microwave relay tower surrounded by a fence. The views here were partially restored by a recently erected observation tower.

The trail down from the summit is a sharp left turn near the telephone line. Your route threads through an attractive field of glacial erratics. After .3 mile, turn left on the yellow-blazed tote road. (The blue Shenipsit Trail continues to the Massachusetts border about six miles further on.)

The yellow trail describes a shallow bowl with a bent lip. You go up the lip, dip gently into the bowl with its swampy bottom, and rise gently to the junction with the blue trail. Proceed straight ahead on the blue trail, retracing your steps 1.6 miles to your car.

19 Newgate Prison

Total distance: 4 miles
Hiking time: 2½ hours/Rating: C
Highlights: Historic Newgate Prison, views

Choose a cool, clear day for this hike. It begins with a pleasant walk along the traprock ridge of the northern Metacomet Trail, then descends into the valley to explore the forbidding environs of infamous Newgate Prison, and finally returns to the start along a well-shaded country road. The views are best when the leaves are off the trees, but you miss the prison unless you venture this way in summer or early autumn.

To reach the hike's start, follow CT 20 west .7 mile from its junction with CT 187 in Granby to Newgate Road, on the right. There is room to park at the corner.

Walk down Newgate Road a few yards, and turn right into the woods on the blue-blazed Metacomet Trail. The path climbs steeply onto the traprock ridge and then bears left along the top.

In leafless seasons the views here are particularly nice, but even in summer you can glimpse the countryside below through occasional breaks in the trees. The utility line you soon pass beneath services a string of ridgetop beacons, a set of signals for planes approaching Bradley International Airport just to the east. The airplane buff will appreciate the steady stream

View from the Metacomet Trail

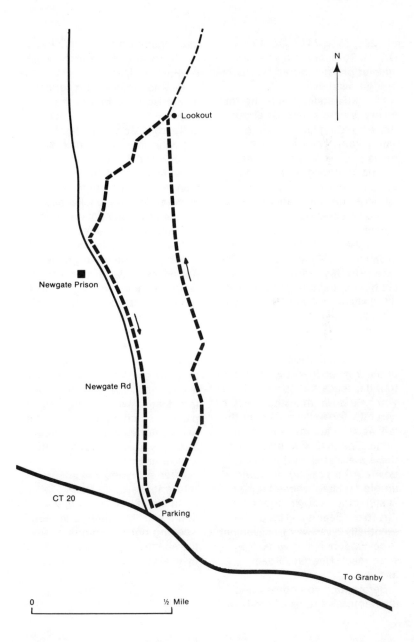

of 727s, 737s, 747s, DC-10s, DC-8s, 707s, and a myriad of smaller private aircraft that come and go overhead.

In a little under 1 mile the trail emerges onto a lookout about three hundred feet above the valley floor. The benchmark reads Copper Mountain. The Tunxis Trail follows the ridge directly opposite you; to your left stretches the sinuous curve of the volcanic ridge the Metacomet Trail follows. Heublein Tower (see Hike 34) stands out prominently; Penwood State Park (see Hike 16) straddles the nearest hump; and past the tower the tilted slabs of Mount Higby (see Hike 33) rise on the far horizon.

Still on the ridge, the trail descends slowly and steadily and then climbs again. Just under 2 miles from the start, the trail descends a second time. As you hike down this slope, watch carefully for white blazes on the left which mark the way off the ridge. The path is obscure, but there are blazes all the way down. After passing the ruins of an old building whose fireplace is still intact, you emerge on a dirt road. Bear left. The dirt eventually gives way to pavement —developers are at work. You soon reach Newgate Road; turn left.

Before long you come upon the impressive ruins of old New-gate Prison on the right. Originally the site of the first copper smelter in America (c. 1705), the mine was pressed into service as a prison just before the Revolutionary War. It is open daily from Memorial Day through October; there is a small fee.

For a short excursion into a seamier side of the nation's past, join the line of waiting visitors. Your daypacks may amuse or astonish many and, perhaps, hearten a few. The idea of the American tourist wedded to his car is deeply ingrained but not necessarily permanent!

After descending 50 feet in a narrow shaft, you enter the mine. Water seeps down the walls. A motley crew of Tories, thieves, and debtors were forced to live and labor in this cavernous prison while fettered with leg irons, handcuffs, and iron collars. Marks worn on the floor by pacing prisoners are still visible two centuries later, and tales of barbarity seem to echo in the hollow chambers.

After exploring the prison, return to Newgate Road. The fresh air will be especially welcome after the dusty dungeon. Keeping right, continue down the shaded, open road for a little over 1 mile to your car.

20 Mount Misery

Total distance: 5¼ miles
Hiking time: 2¾ hours/Rating: CD
Highlights: Views, rhododendron and cedar swamp

Rhododendron

The delightful little summit of
Mount Misery belies its name.
Set amidst flat pinelands of Connecticut's largest state forest,
this prominent rocky mass adds
a nice short climb to an otherwise level hike. Your route to the
top, where there are nice views
across wooded terrain, follows
the Nehantic Trail. This hike picks
up the Nehantic Trail on CT 49 in
Voluntown. From the intersection
of CT 49, CT 165, and CT 138,
head east on CT 165 to CT 49
north and turn left. The blue
blazes of the trail run along the
road, veering sharply left into the
woods .6 mile from the junction.
Park here off the highway.

As you enter the woods, even
rows of white and red pine
stretch away on either side. The
conifers begin to thin out and
are replaced by short, scrubby,
head-high bushes of bear oak.
These trees flourish (if that word
may be used for these scraggly
specimens) in dry, barren soil.
Less tolerant but more vigorous
trees prevent them from gaining
a foothold in richer soil.

Nearly ½ mile from the start
the Pachaug enters on the right,
and the two trails continue as
one over Mount Misery. The way
is marked by an apparently
excessive number of blue blazes.
The combination of trails and an
open picnic area just ahead has
caused great confusion among

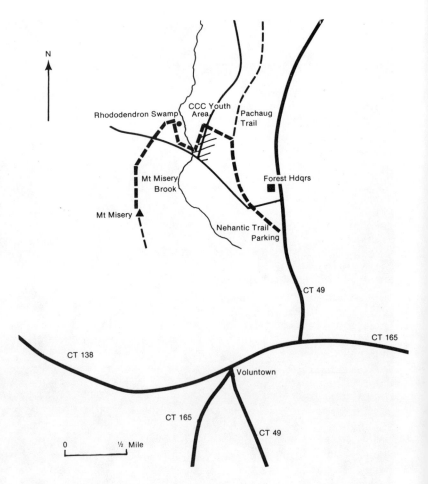

hikers in the past — hence the plethora of markings.

As you come out of the woods, an arrow painted on a large, heavily branched white pine directs you left down into the CCC Youth Area, a recreational site with picnic tables, fireplaces, and outhouses. The trail cuts through the field toward some apple trees, passes by stone gates, crosses a tar road by the campground sign, and then joins another tar road to bridge Mount Misery Brook. To your right a footbridge leads to a picnic table attractively situated on a small island in midstream. The trail soon breaks to the right off the road and passes through a grove of young white oaks.

Presently you drop down into a cedar and rhododendron swamp; you appreciate the dry, raised trail bed here. Along this stretch of the swamp, junglelike rhododendron flank the trail. This evergreen can grow surprisingly tall — to forty feet — and its leathery leaves can reach eight inches in length. The combined effect of all that green is most impressive. In July the huge bushes are dotted with white or pink bell-shaped flowers, creating a spectacular display. Here and there the straight, even boles of tall white cedar thrust through the mass. Their bark is soft and flaky; the greenish tint

you see is algae growing on the trees' damp surfaces.

Emerging from the swamp, the trail intersects a tote road. Turn left. The blazes are plentiful at the junction, but they are not always easy to spot among the evergreen shrubbery. In less than ¼ mile and just before a small pond on the left, the trail bears right off the tote road.

Before you turn, stop and listen. On one mid-March hike here the warm sun beating down on the pond had aroused the resident wood frogs, despite the residue from a recent snowfall. Their full gutteral chorus was broken only by the plaintive "peep" of a solitary spring peeper too groggy to give the second half of his familiar call.

The level trail passes through oaks and hemlocks. A blue-blazed white cedar with a split down the center large enough to see through stands right in the middle of the trail. What caused this hole? Did two trees grow together? One of the pleasures of hiking is trying to figure out how such strange phenomena occurred.

The path climbs now, gently at first, to the top of a ridge. Turn right. A singularly mis-shapen, wind-twisted scrub pine grows on the ledge lookout. Below you can see open fields where snowmobiles congregate

in the winter.

The trail soon drops a bit before making its final assault up Mount Misery. The bolts and guy wires you see in the ledges at the top used to support a fire tower that was abandoned in the mid-1970s. Although Mount Misery, at 441 feet, is not very high, the summit provides a fine view. Voluntown lies to the far right.

On a calm day the open summit ledges also make a fine picnic spot. Be sure to carry your garbage out with you as you retrace your steps to your car.

21 Wolf Den

Total distance: 5 miles
Hiking time: 2¾ hours/Rating: CD
Highlights: Wolf den, Indian chair, state park

The Indian chair

Some words roll off the tongue with melodious grace. Although Mashamoquet (mash-muk-it) Brook is definitely not one of those, this state park has a special beauty and grace due to its botanical and zoological diversity. You also find nestled in its 781 acres the legendary wolf den where Israel Putnam, a general of Revolutionary War fame, reputedly shot the last wolf in Connecticut. We could easily have devoted many more pages to this particular hike.

From the junction of CT 101 and US 44 in Pomfret, head south on Wolf Den Drive for .7 mile. Turn left into the Mashamoquet overflow camping area, where there is ample parking.

To reach the blue-blazed trail that loops past the wolf den and Indian chair, walk back down the gravel road and cross Wolf Den Drive. The trail starts through a stone wall where "Mashamoquet" has been painted in yellow on a rock. The blazes lead you across an old field and then turn left into a large stand of smooth alder. Here skunk cabbages spread their large leaves across the shaded, swampy ground. Within the thicket the hulk of a great black willow is matching its vigor against the dissolution of age.

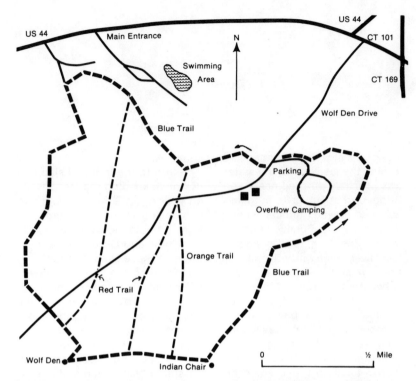

When you reach the edge of a cornfield, turn left by the shagbark hickory and enter the woods. These first few hundred yards from the start provide a wonderful illustration of the successive stages in the development of a mature forest. You passed first the open field, next the swamp-nurtured invading alder grove, and then cleared wasteland with juniper and young red cedar. These trees are among the first to colonize open spaces. The forest is further advanced in the woods you have just entered; here large red cedars are losing the battle for sunlight to the taller, faster growing birches. In time these trees will be crowded out by oaks, the climax forest in this part of the state.

Beyond a small stream several large, plate-barked black birches guard the trail, which soon runs parallel to a stone wall. Where the stone wall turns a corner the trail joins a tote road. A red-blazed path goes left, cutting across the blue loop trail, but you bear right with the blue blazes on the level tote road through a maturing oak and maple woods. Stay right on the blue and red trail (the blazes are together) until the blue forks left. (The red trail continues to the right across trout-stocked Mashamoquet Brook to the picnic and swimming area.)

Your route curves left through the woods, crosses a stream over an old bridge, and starts up a deeply eroded old road. Soon you should spot the cement arrow directing you left off the road. Several of these nearly vandal-proof arrows provide directions at key junctions throughout the park. (The old road continues a short distance to the main campground road; according to many campers, the pump there has the "best water in Connecticut.")

The trail moves up a gentle slope through large hardwoods and continues left along an open hayfield. It is easy to let your mind wander as your feet take you down worn old roads such as this one; we still miss marked turns after thousands of miles of hiking experience.

The trail levels and then meets a gravel road. Turn right and then left almost immediately on another gravel road, passing between a pair of well-built stone cairns. Each cairn contains a large stone with the chiseled words "Wolf Den Entrance" highlighted with yellow paint.

Follow the dirt road past thick clumps of laurel to a parking area with a few picnic tables nearby. Continue through the lot to the back of a small circular drive and proceed downhill. Soon the red trail comes in from the left by a cement arrow. The red and blue trails now drop together steeply into the valley below on impressive stone steps. Less than halfway down, you reach the fabled wolf den.

It was here in 1742, according to legend, that Israel Putnam slew the last wolf in Connecticut. In fact, the last wolf in the state was probably downed near Bridgeport about 1840. Putnam's wolf had preyed on local sheep for some years. Finally, after tracking her from the Connecticut River some thirty-five miles to the west, the intrepid Putnam crawled into the den with a lantern, saw the burning eyes of the trapped beast, backed out, grabbed his musket, crawled in again, and fired. Temporarily deafened, he backed out of the smoke-filled hole, paused, went in a third time, and hauled out the carcass.

As you peek inside, note the weathered initials chiseled on the sides of the den entrance. In the last century such graffitti was laboriously etched on the rocks; today's vandals use paint cans.

When you finish examining the den, continue down the slope. The red blazes break off to the left, but you follow the blue ones across Wolf Den Brook and climb the sloping ledges on the other side. Past the crest of a rounded hill, an orange-blazed trail comes in on the left. A short distance beyond, the trail bears left on the slope; here you go right a few feet to a ledge overlook and the Indian chair. An appropriately shaped boulder, the chair commands a fine view of the surrounding countryside.

Return to the trail and slab left downhill, keeping the stone wall on your right. Shining club moss perches on some of the fern-framed boulders; wood ferns, polypody, and Christmas fern thrive in these shady woods.

Now climb the boulder-strewn hill ahead. The slope is softened near the top by a carpet of white pine needles. After dipping and hesitating slightly, the trail curves right up a rocky draw, turns right, and descends again, passing a black birch and a hemlock embraced in mortal combat for the same piece of ground. To your right the evergreen sterile fronds of the maidenhair spleenwort are lodged in the cracks of a large seamed bolder. The fertile fronds unfold in the spring and die with the first frost.

The trail bends right and then zigzags down the hillside, crossing a stone wall before skirting the edge of the field that borders the overflow camping area where you started. Nature loves edges. Edges provide habitats for plants that can stand neither full sun nor full shade. Wild animals use the woods for cover and feed on the field plants and border shrubs.

Soon the trail curves back into the woods along a beaver-flooded swamp. Part way around, a board pier goes out into the water for close observation. We scared up a great blue heron here. This long-necked bird with a six-foot wing span uses its long legs to keep its plumage above shallow water. As he wades, his sharp-pointed beak unerringly spears small fish, frogs, and other aquatic life.

After circling the lower field, the trail cuts across the upper field to a clump of white pines complete with picnic table and adjacent putting green(!). Passing through the pine grove, the trail curves right to the dirt track through the camping area to your car.

22 Northern Nipmuck

Total distance: 5¼ miles
Hiking time: 3 hours/Rating: C
Highlights: Wild wooded area

Black-eyed susans at a field's edge

The entire 14-mile section of the
northern Nipmuck Trail dedicated
in May, 1976, makes for delightful
woods walking. This hike samples
only 4 miles of this recent addition
to Connecticut's Blue Trail system, and then returns you to
your start along two little-used
gravel roads with the unusual
names of Boston Hollow Road
and Axe Factory Road.

The start of this hike is located
in northern Connecticut where
the crisscrossed roads are as
independent as their inhabitants.
Follow CT 89 north 4 miles from
the junction of US 44 and CT 89
in Warrenville. Bear right at the
Westford traffic light. In .3 mile,
where the tar road bends right,
stay straight on gravel Boston
Hollow Road. Watch carefully —
the blue-blazed trail crosses in
1.3 miles. There is enough room
for two cars to park on the left.

Follow the blazes north (left)
into the woods. In late summer
the flat forest floor is liberally
decorated with Virginia creeper,
wild sarsaparilla, fruiting blue
cohosh, and interrupted and rattlesnake ferns. The last is the
largest and most common of the
succulent grape ferns; the
simple, large, triangular leaf and
the early season spore stalk are
unmistakable.

Shortly the trail climbs steeply
onto a hemlock- and oak-
covered ridge and bends left.

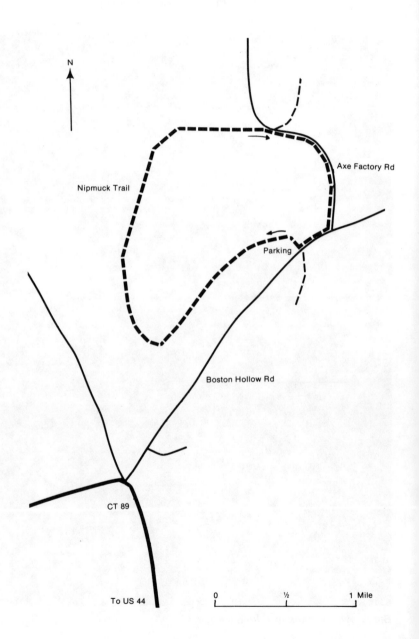

N

Nipmuck Trail

Axe Factory Rd

Parking

Boston Hollow Rd

CT 89

To US 44

0   ½   1 Mile

Boston Hollow Road, parallel to the trail, is visible below through the trees. Then, winding to the right through thickets of mountain laurel, the path slabs a hemlock-covered hillside. Although the hiker finds laurel lovely — in winter the evergreen leaves add color to the woods and in spring there is no more beautiful blossom — its tangled growth is the bane of the trail clearer. It is a tough, stubborn bush whose cut-off stubs have to be removed lest they trip and impale the careless hiker.

Jouncing up and down several small rocky ridges, you pass scattered patches of striped maple. If you walk this way in mid-August, you can just catch the first signs of a tipping of the year's hourglass. The lush vegetation of summer looks slightly shopworn. Evergreen plants, previously overshadowed, sparkle with a fresh sheen that will carry through fall and winter and into yet another spring. Goldenrods and asters are prominent. The fall spate of mushrooms have started: white and yellowish puffballs, white amanitas that only the experts dare sort and eat (the deadliest is appropriately named the destroying angel!), and the red-capped, emetic russala. Moss-bedded dry rocky rills recall spring's wetness. Here the ghostly Indian pipes have become blackened skeletons although they may be just erupting in the mountains to the north. The false hellebore or Indian poke, here quite shriveled, similarly still flowers above tree line in northern New England. A lover of particular flowers can prolong the viewing season by moving north with the blooms. Likewise, if you zig when you should have zagged, you may miss some short-seasoned flower altogether.

In about 2¾ miles, you cross an old dirt road pointedly labeled "Private Drive" in both directions. Such signs are a reminder that many trails are ours to use only as long as *all* hikers treat the private property that the trails cross with special care. About ½ mile farther on, you ascend a hemlock-covered escarpment; below is one of Bigelow Brook's small, turbulent, noisy tributaries.

In another ½ mile or so, after bearing left downhill, you emerge on gravel Axe Factory Road by a stream-threaded meadow. Although the woods vegetation is faded, late summer sees a riotous flowering in open fields and meadows. Great purple-crowned stalks of Joe-Pye weed, white-flowering boneset (an herbal fever remedy), goldenrods, St. Johnswort, three-leaved hog peanut vines, and pealike clusters of ground-nuts are everywhere. Blackberries invite you to snack, bumblebees engage in a final orgy of nectar gathering, and the smell of pepperbush pervades the area. Here the marshy stream trickles through metal culverts, and minnows and pickerel play deadly hide-and-seek amid the waterweeds.

You are just under 1¼ miles from your car. Leaving the trail behind, return to your car by following Axe Factory Road to the right and then Boston Hollow Road, also to the right. Both these gravel roads are little used and a delight to walk. Cement and stone remnants of a mill wall are visible from the next bridge. Pasturing cows and a farm pond farther on compose a peaceful scene — a fitting conclusion to a relaxing hike in the countryside.

23 Dean Ravine and Barrack Mountain

Total distance: 3.8 miles
Hiking time: 2½ hours/Rating: B
Highlights: Ravine, cascade, views

Considerable ups and downs are necessary to combine the two very different but delightful attractions of this hike in western Connecticut. If the day is hot, the ravine will cool you; if it is cold, the sun-drenched ledges of the mountain will warm you. Some people might regard this less favorably and say that in any weather you'll be uncomfortable at least part of the day, but hikers should always look on the bright side. After all, the forests and mountain tops have a special beauty in each season and every type of weather.

The hike starts by Dean Ravine. From the junction of CT 112 and US 7 in Salisbury, drive east on US 7 across the river. In .3 mile, turn right on Warren Turnpike. In .9 mile, take a left on Music Mountain Road. Where it meets Cream Hill Road in .9 mile, there is a sizable parking lot on your left. Several picnic tables, a trash barrel, and an outhouse are here for your convenience.

At the very edge of the woods near the outhouse, we discovered a large patch of mayapples. Standing a foot or so high and shaped like large umbrellas with deeply cut leaves and white blossoms, these exotic-looking plants are

In Dean Ravine

uncommon in New England. To date, the edge of this ravine is the only place we've seen them in Connecticut. The mayapple spreads by creeping rhizomes, so when it does grow it is usually found in large patches. Although the leaves and roots are poisonous, the insipid fruits which ripen in July are edible but can be a strong cathartic.

Before leaving the parking area, look to the middle of the adjacent grove of red pines for a rather scraggly specimen whose upper trunk is composed of an orange brown, flaky bark. This tree is not red pine with a mysterious blight but the alien Scotch pine recently in great demand as a Christmas tree. For some reason Scotch pines that grow in the East are often misshapen.

Now drop down into Dean Ravine on the white-blazed Appalachian Trail (AT), which slants left from the parking area. There are some nice falls and cascades a short distance upstream. Dean Ravine is especially cool in the heat of summer. The trail heads downstream, leveling off while the stream at right drops away. Take a few minutes to walk over to see the roaring water and falls, where the stream is narrowed by hard rock walls. Then return to the trail, which zigzags down to the

stream, and admire the cascade from the bottom.

A short side trail leads right, away from the AT to the foot of the cascade. From below, the narrow passage through which the water gushes is sharply etched. Mosses color the damp edges of the ledges, and hemlocks cling to the steep, rugged sides where violets add spots of bright color.

Return to the trail and edge down the stream. Climb over rocks and logs as the trail undulates along the stream. The trail enters a glen filled with fascinatingly beautiful ferns. There are delicate maidenhairs with their radiating circlet of fronds on thin, black, wiry stems; circular clumps of cinnamon ferns surrounding the cinnamon brown fertile leaves with their light brown tufts of wool; and the large, graceful, arching plumes of the ostrich fern whose fronds steadily widen then narrow rapidly to a blunt point at the tip.

In about .6 mile the trail angles away from the stream onto Music Mountain Road, which it follows right for .1 mile. In spring white blackberry blossoms by the roadside presage late summer's juicy fruit. The apparent spring asters are actually common daisy fleabane, so called because when burned the smoke is supposed to drive

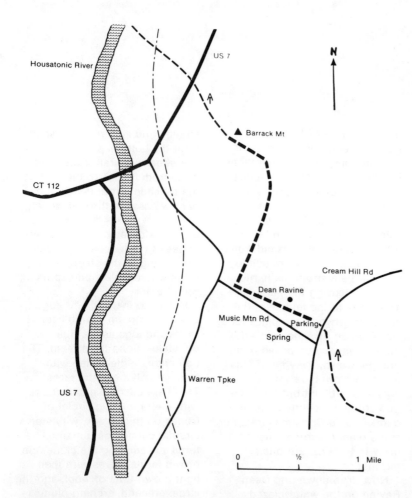

Housatonic River

US 7

N

▲ Barrack Mt

CT 112

Cream Hill Rd

Dean Ravine

Music Mtn Rd — Parking

Spring

Warren Tpke

US 7

0   ½   1 Mile

As you come out onto open ledges you begin to catch glimpses of sights to come. About 1.2 miles from the road you reach Lookout Point. While not the summit of Barrack Mountain, it is far and away the best viewpoint. Ledges drop away in front of you in giant steps; pines have found footholds here and there.

To the far right twists the oval of Lime Rock's race track. In season, the whining roar of the cars is a constant accompaniment to your thoughts and conversation; the lull between races is greatly appreciated. Below you the Housatonic River glints through the trees. On both banks you can distinguish open fields and fields dotted with red cedars —no monotony of uniformity here. To your left, on the east bank of the river, the vegetation forms a solid geometrical formation; that stand of evergreens, probably red pine, has been planted.

If the sun is warm and the breeze pleasant, take a nap and enjoy your surroundings. Then retrace your steps back through the ravine to your car. Before you leave the parking area search out the ice-cold piped spring on the left about 150 yards down Music Mountain Road.

away insects.

Just after you cross the bridge bear right into the woods, climbing the steep bank up a rocky ridge. As you rise, watch for ebony spleenwort, a tiny fern with narrow fronds cut into unpaired leaflets with eared upper sides. The sterile leaves are evergreen while the stalks are a shiny deep brown. The sun-baked ledges in which they grow provide you with welcome warmth in cold

weather but double your discomfort in summer.

The trail drops steeply down to the base of Barrack Mountain, crosses an ice-cold rill, and starts up again. You climb steadily over oak- and hickory-covered slopes. Although the rise is not long, the steepness of the ledges makes this section difficult—be careful climbing here and be even more cautious on the way down.

24 Green Falls Pond

Total distance: 5.7 miles
Hiking time: 3 hours/Rating: CD
Highlights: Ravine, secluded pond, state park

Green Falls Pond

Far eastern Connecticut seems to have been forgotten by the twentieth century. Roads go from tar to dirt, and stone walls are strikingly square and straight, evidence that they are not the trappings of gentleman farmers but functional components of working farms. Except for occasional fields and farmhouses, this untenanted, overgrown area is much as the westward-bound pioneers left it. Our hike on the Narragansett Trail to Green Falls Pond takes you through this secluded region.

From the junction of CT 49, CT 138, and CT 165 in Voluntown, drive south on CT 49 for 4 miles and turn left on Sand Hill Road. In just under 1 mile, take Wheeler Road on the right for .4 mile until you see the blue blazes of the Narragansett Trail crossing. Park beyond the blazes, pulling as far off the road as possible; the traffic is minimal.

Enter the woods on the left (east) side of the road by the small circular state forest emblem. The trail rolls gently downward with many seasonal streams interrupting the path and soothing the soul with their melodious chatter. This thin-soiled, rock-ribbed land is largely clothed in oak.

In .4 mile the trail proceeds down a steep rocky slope toward the valley, crossing a stream and skirting the left side of a swamp. On your left you pass a twenty-five-foot-high rock face graced with lichens, mosses, and even a few trees. Just beyond is a more impressive rock face with larger trees growing from its sides. At its base lies a jumble of large rock slabs that were once part of the cliff. Perhaps they were forced off in years past by trees, since vanished, whose incessant growth slowly but surely splits rock.

You cross another stream to the edge of Green Falls River valley by a large, crumbling boulder. Look closely at this rock mass; its shade, moisture retention, and thrust toward the sun create miniature ecosystems. While the stark, drier sides are gray with lichens, the shaded areas with pockets of soil hold soft moss cushions. In wet times the surface of a moist, crumbly hollow is colored with light green algae. The thin soil of its horizontal surfaces supports clumps of polypody fern. Large birches buttress the sides of the boulder, which is crowned with an out-of-place juniper; the rock's sunny, well-drained top provides the conditions the juniper needs. An early settler of untended fields, this prickly evergreen is ordinarily shaded out by taller successional trees.

The trail angles left, crossing two rocky seasonal streams. Step carefully; the rough surfaced rocks become very slippery when their covering of mosses and lichens swells with moisture. After the second stream, proceed gradually uphill and along the valley rim to Green Falls Road, a dirt road 1.4 miles from your start.

Take the road right, downhill, for .1 mile. After crossing the bridge, turn left and follow the river upstream. The path now climbs a rocky ledge before slipping down into a narrow ravine which speeds the river over boulders and ledges. You again cross the river, this time on a plank footbridge.

The trail clambers over boulders where root-hung hemlocks cling to a steep, eroding slope and then bypasses two rather rotten logs spanning the river. The inward-pressing rock walls are thickly covered with mosses and lichens. Soon the trail climbs steeply up the side of the hill to avoid a sheer drop into the river. Be careful not to trip on the exposed roots along the top.

You reach the base of the Green Falls Pond dam in 1.9 miles. The water tumbles down its face as individually protruding rocks create a multiplicity of small cascades. Cross the bridge and climb to the top of the dam.

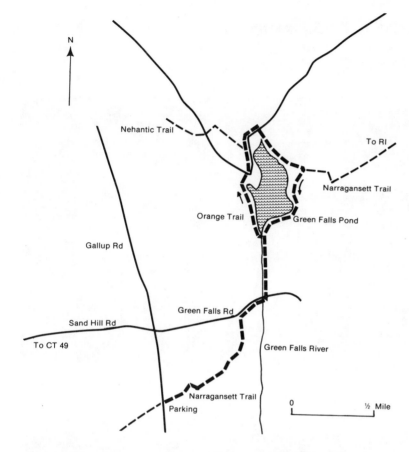

N

Nehantic Trail

To RI

Narragansett Trail

Orange Trail

Green Falls Pond

Gallup Rd

Green Falls Rd

Sand Hill Rd

To CT 49

Green Falls River

Narragansett Trail
Parking

0   ½ Mile

orange-blazed trail continues along the park entrance road before turning right uphill. Ledge outcroppings are covered with a large, thick-fleshed, curling lichen called rock tripe, which is considered nourishing in case of dire emergency. Canadian voyageurs reputedly used it to thicken their soups.

The trail is now in sight of the pond. The orange trail ends at the blue-blazed Narragansett Trail 1.2 miles from the dam; turn right. Cross a small brook on stepping stones; in high water an upstream detour will let you cross dryshod.

The trail climbs a rocky ridge for the view of nearby rolling hills, drops down, and visits a rocky point. Enjoy these meanderings — a well laid-out trail is properly concerned with exploring all points of interest — after all, this is why most of us hike. Continue across an earth-filled auxiliary dam. The underwater face is covered with rock riprap to minimize erosion.

The trail enters the woods just beyond the auxiliary dam. Follow the ridge overlooking the pond before descending diagonally down to the shore. Cross the single handrail bridge by the main dam .7 mile from the end of the orange-blazed trail and retrace your steps down the ravine to your starting point.

Here you leave the blue-blazed Narragansett Trail for an alternate orange-blazed trail, which goes around the west side of Green Falls Pond. This trout-stocked pond is one of the nicest in Connecticut; it has lovely ledges dropping into the water, small islands, fully wooded shores, and no cottages.

The trail hugs a shore thickly grown with laurel, oak, birch, and hemlock. About .2 mile from the dam the path crosses a feeder stream and continues rounding the pond. If you lose the trail here, head toward the pond — in most places the trail edges the shore. As you advance, picnic tables come into view (many are of massive log construction). A ledge-tipped point to the right is the closest approach to the pond's largest island.

Soon you reach the gravel road that services the state park. The pump on the left provides good drinking water. The

25 Great Hill

Total distance: 5½ miles
Hiking time: 3 hours/Rating: C
Highlights: Cobalt mine, view, cascade

This hike begins on the Shenipsit Trail near a long-abandoned cobalt mine in the obscure town of Cobalt. From there, you climb a rocky ridge to Great Hill, which rewards you with a panoramic view over the Connecticut River. A short hike along the ridge brings you to a beautiful, secluded cascade at the foot of Bald Hill.

From the junction of CT 66 and CT 151 in Cobalt, drive north on Depot Hill Road. At the first fork keep right up a steep hill. After .8 mile, turn right onto Gadpouch Road. The blue-blazed Shenipsit starts on the left in .5 mile. Park on the right just beyond the trail head.

First walk over to a large hemlock grove shading the ravine to your right. The old mineral diggings lie between you and the stream at the bottom. There is no marked trail down the steep sides. Proceed with caution; numerous deep pits exist where the mine roof has caved in. Originally opened by Governor John Winthrop in 1661, the mine was active from the mid-1700s to the mid-1800s. The cobalt extracted here was shipped as far away as England and China for use in the manufacture of a deep blue paint and porcelain glaze.

Small cave in Great Hill

Return to the trail head across the road and follow the blazes through ash-dominated hardwoods. These trees range from mature specimens two feet in diameter to fast-growing, strong, lightweight sprouts the size of baseball bats. This section of the trail, always wet and muddy, is at its worst during the spring thaw.

The trail starts climbing gradually. Look to the left for the round-leaved shoots of the wild onion. The leaves and bulb provide a sharp-tasting treat. In spring skunk cabbage raises its hooded head above the soggy ground.

Soon the trail climbs steeply and then levels briefly. As you resume climbing, look to the right for a patch of the creeping evergreen, partridgeberry. The tiny, heart-shaped leaves set off any bright red berries that may have been overlooked by ruffed grouse and white-footed wood mice. Oddly, this relative of the dainty bluet thrives in Mexico and Japan as well as in most of eastern North America.

The trail zigzags steeply up the rocky side of Great Hill. At the crest take the yellow-blazed trail left a short distance to the rocky lookout. Follow the Connecticut River with your eye. Directly below you is cottage-rimmed Great Hill Pond. In the middle distance are the smoke stacks of

the Middletown power plants. Next to a girder-framed dock the Pratt and Whitney Middletown Jet Engine Facility sprawls over the countryside. Here barges and small tankers offload their cargos of jet fuel in midriver. Continuing southward, the river's wanderings become lost amidst the horizon's low, rolling hills. The Mattabesett Trail follows the western horizon ridges. Northwest of the power plant the bare slopes of the Powder Ridge Ski Area scar the ridge. The old colonial seaport of Middletown lies on the west side of the river.

Retrace your steps to the blue blazes. The trail runs north-northeast along the straight, narrow ridge for almost 2 miles before descending.

About 1½ miles into the hike, look for an attractive rock jumble capped with evergreen polypody ferns. The deep green leaves of this common shade-loving fern rise from creeping root stalks. It grows on rocks, cliff edges, and even trees where acid humus has accumulated. In midsummer the undersides of the upper leaflets are decorated with double rows of red brown spore bodies.

The trail descends the ridge gradually and joins a tote road in ¼ mile. Used mostly before World War I, tote roads were cut to "tote" logs from the woods. The soil was so compacted

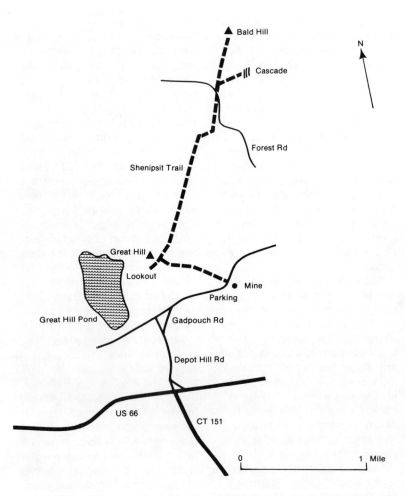

minor differences of soil or exposure can create these distinct demarcation lines. The large, tuliplike orange and green flowers and distinctive four-pointed leaves with a notched tip are unmistakable in summer. The numerous flower husks clinging to upper branches are a sure winter identification.

After ¼ mile follow another tote road to the right. Cross a brook; shortly the trail leaves the tote road, right, and immediately turns right, following yellow blazes for about 100 yards to a cascade.

This is one of our favorite places. In spring the sheet of water flowing evenly down the steep face of a moss-covered rock ledge creates a soothing sound. Bubbles formed in the turbulence glide merrily across the pool beneath, forming windrows of pollution-free foam. This is a fine place for a quiet picnic, a good book, or simply a restful interlude.

If you want a bit more exercise (or a more exposed picnic spot), return to the blue blazes, turn right, and climb ¼ mile to the top of Bald Hill. There is no view here.

When you are ready, retrace your steps—perhaps pausing for a final view from the Great Hill lookout before returning to your car.

from logging operations that many of these old lanes are still virtually free of vegetation.

After another ¼ mile the trail joins a gravel forest road. As you cross to the west-facing slope, notice the scattered, straight, tall tulip trees that were absent from the east-facing slope. Here, near the tulip tree's northern limit,

26 Devil's Hopyard

Total distance: 4.5 miles
Hiking time: 3 hours/Rating: CB
Highlights: Cascade, falls, impressive trees, views

View to Eight Mile River valley

Water dominates the 860-acre Devil's Hopyard: water in the form of the rushing, turbulent Eight Mile River and its tributaries; water as the agent that gave shape to much of this ragged, scenic area. Throughout the state park, you pass beneath groves of great trees, primarily hemlock, with wide boles, straight trunks, and first limbs twenty or more feet above the ground. They create a brush-free setting for your explorations.

The Devil's Hopyard became a state park in 1919. The origin of its colorful name is lost in a welter of fanciful stories ranging from the simple corruption of Mr. Dibble's hopyard to tales of mist-shrouded forms seen dancing on the ledges.

From the junction of CT 82 and CT 156 in East Haddam, drive east .1 mile on CT 82 to Hopyard Road and turn left (north). Follow this road 3 miles to the park entrance and turn right. At the bottom of the hill, bear left to one of several parking areas. This park is fully developed, with picnic tables, fireplaces, rainy weather shelters, and fifteen miles of hiking trails.

Cross the river (liberally stocked with trout) through the picturesque covered footbridge. Immediately turn left and follow the yellow blazes along the river bank to the Flume, a dry water chute.

From here you can see both Chapman Falls on the left and a series of lesser unnamed falls on the right. Since Chapman Falls are more accessible from the other side of the river, save them for the end of your hike. For a look at the lesser falls, cross a small bridge over a tributary stream. The falls area contains many signs of circular erosion, including another smooth, dry chute to the left.

Now retrace your steps to the trail junction and turn left on the yellow-blazed Tablet Rock Trail. Across the next bridge, fork right (the path straight leads to Foxtown Road) along the stream's north bank. As you bend away from the falls and climb a hill covered with laurel, look left to the stepped escarpment. Protruding layers of hard caprock overlie layers of softer, less-resistant rock; without this combination, the falls would degenerate into tumbling rapids.

Farther on a large, dead hemlock stands to your left. This decaying hulk nourishes great insect colonies, which in turn feed innumerable birds. A woodland swept clean of dead and dying overmature trees such as this one is a wildlife desert!

Cross, in order, the left branch of the brook, the Loop Trail, and the larger right branch of the brook. Proceed uphill through pines; then continue along a down-sloping plateau. Soon you pass a huge white oak with pocked, unhealthy bark. This tree is in the last stages of dissolution. One whole side has split off (lightning?), exposing an enormous decaying scar. Great bands of rounded new growth flank the gash; in vain, the great oak tried to cover its decaying heartwood, now freckled with fungal, fruiting bodies and riddled with dry rot. Most of its great limbs have fallen; a few green leaves are its only sign of life. The surrounding thick stand of young hemlocks is the forest's response to the flood of sunlight released by the dying patriarch.

The trail continues down the slope along a small, seasonal trickle to the edge of a steep drop. Keep sharply left along the rim. After .4 mile, a yellow arrow painted on a tree directs you sharply right. You soon reach a footpath that breaks to the left off the main trail. Follow this path downhill for about 150 yards to a rocky outcropping on the edge of a steep drop.

The Eight Mile River valley lies below you. Hemlocks march down the steep hillsides. The dammed remains of a pond form the centerpiece of your view, and directly beyond, a single farm and field breaks the undulating blanket of treetops. A closer look shows that the field is an alluvial

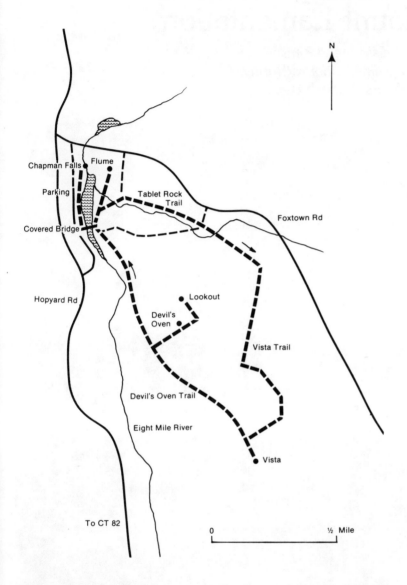

N

Chapman Falls
Flume
Parking
Tablet Rock Trail
Covered Bridge
Foxtown Rd
Hopyard Rd
Lookout
Devil's Oven
Vista Trail
Devil's Oven Trail
Eight Mile River
Vista
To CT 82

0   ½ Mile

is a small, shallow cave—the Devil's Oven. Continuing around and up to the right, you reach another overlook with valley views.

Retrace your steps carefully to the main trail, again heading right along the river. Shortly, the trail bears slightly right, away from the river, and ascends a stepped ledge to a hemlock-covered flat. It then runs gently down to the covered footbridge you passed over at the start. Cross the bridge and head to the right, upriver, to Chapman Falls.

For over a century prior to its inclusion in the state park, this sixty-foot waterfall powered a mill. The sheets of water now drop freely in a series of falls and cascades. After admiring them from below, curve left on the trail up to a graded path and turn right to reach the top of the falls. Be careful here; the wet rocks, long drops, and thundering water are potentially dangerous.

In summer the decreased water volume is counter-balanced by the exposure of numerous potholes. These circular holes in solid ledge are caused by loose rocks caught and circulated in depressions by the rushing water.

When ready, retrace your steps down the graded path to your car.

fan. Eroding water tore this material from the hills behind it and, when the current slowed, dropped the debris in a fan-shaped area, flattening the valley floor.

Retrace your steps to the main trail, watching carefully for the junction, and head left downhill. The trail bears right toward the river. Follow it upstream until you arrive at a large yellow arrow that points to the right.

A short, scrambling ascent up a steep slope leads you to a rock outcropping. Set in the rock face

27 Chauncey Peak and Mount Lamentation

Total distance: 4.8 miles
Hiking time: 3 hours/Rating: B
Highlights: Superb views

The traprock ridges within the Connecticut River valley are a hiker's paradise. Ascents are steep and rugged, while views from the cliff edges are superb. This hike along a section of the Mattabesett Trail is one of the best of the traprock cliffs and offers a panoramic view within the first .3 mile. Climb Chauncey Peak and Mount Lamentation on a cool, clear day and you won't be disappointed.

From I-91 near Meriden, take exit 20 to Country Club Road. Follow this road west about 3 miles. Since Country Club Road connects the trails to Mount Higby (see Hike 33) and Chauncey Peak, blue blazes appear occasionally on the telephone poles. The blue-blazed Mattabesett Trail turns right into the woods at a sharp left curve .5 mile beyond a traprock quarry. A wide shoulder offers ample room for parking.

As you enter the woods you pass a large bed of gill-over-the-ground, a small plant with tiny, tubular purple flowers. This member of the mint family was once used to ferment beer. Shortly you come across patches of wild onion—flavor for your sandwiches—and silverweed.

Looking south from Mt. Lamentation to the Sleeping Giant

Gerry first identified silverweed, which looks like a many-leaved strawberry plant, in Newfoundland, and we've since spotted it several times in Connecticut. This illustrates the value of recognition; once you have identified a plant, you notice it where you never realized it existed.

The trail soon starts to climb, becoming steadily steeper and rockier. Many flowering dogwoods light the forest's middle story along the way. After hiking .3 mile, you finally pass through almost sheer traprock ramparts and emerge on the level top of Chauncey Peak (688 feet). The southern panorama is very special.

New Haven and the faint blue line of Long Island lie straight ahead. The lumpy mass to their right is the Sleeping Giant (see Hike 42) and then West Rock ridge (see Hike 50). Directly right stretch the Hanging Hills of Meriden; South Mountain partially blocks Castle Crag and West Peak (see Hike 49). To your left rise the cliffs of Mount Higby.

All these ridges are composed of traprock formed some 200 million years ago. Most are remnants of vast, upended lava sheets, but a few, such as West Rock ridge, are exposed lava dikes.

The trail tracks east along the southern cliff edge, and then turns left to meander across the top to the western cliffs. The trees you pass are predominantly chestnut oak and staghorn sumac, two species that can tolerate the thin, dry soil on the crest. As you reach the edge, the view south looks down on a traprock quarry. (The hard, crushed stone is an ideal highway base.)

The vistas from these cliffs are among the finest in the state; as you work your way along the edge, rocky outcroppings provide unobstructed views of Crescent Lake, 300 feet directly beneath you. From the final outcrop, the vista sweeps from New Haven west past the Hanging Hills and north past the Hartford skyline to the hills crossed by the northern section of the Shenipsit Trail (see Hike 18).

The trail drops off Chauncey Peak, crosses a brook .8 mile from the start, and heads up a wide, rocky path. Following the blue blazes, bear left at the fork and left again when you reach the tote road. In a few yards the blazes lead to the right back into the woods. Climbing steadily uphill, you curve around the southern end of Mount Lamentation (720 feet) and come out on the western cliffs of this ridge, 1.4 miles from the start.

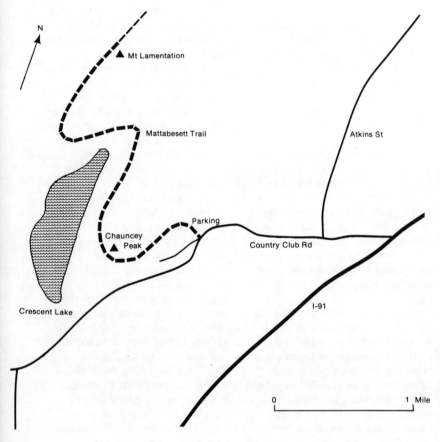

While taking an unmarked detour through the woods here, we came across a fearless black rat snake. This one was 4½ feet long, an average length for this species. (They regularly grow to 6 feet.) Unfortunately, these and many other helpful, rodent-catching snakes have become scarce of late from wanton killing. This one let Gerry lift it gently off the ground so we could see the underside checkerboard pattern that distinguishes it from the similar but more common black racer. How easily a misguided person could have killed it!

The trail parallels the cliffs for almost 1 mile and ends with a particularly fine view that extends from New Haven to Hartford and beyond. On a clear day you can identify the traprock ridges north of Springfield, Massachusetts. From left to right, the east-facing cliffs of Mount Tom are followed by the gap cut by the Connecticut River, the multi-summited Holyoke Range, and finally Mount Norwottuck. This last peak marks where the emergent traprock disappears into overlying red sandstone.

After a leisurely lunch, retrace your steps to your car.

All-Day Hikes

28 Bolton Notch

Total distance: 6 miles
Hiking time: 3½ hours/Rating: CD
Highlights: Rock-cut railroad bed, pond

Along the old railroad bed in Bolton Notch

You should be confident of your ability to scout unmarked paths before attempting this hike. The first half of this loop hike tends north along an abandoned railroad bed and presents no problems, but the return route wends through the woods on various unmarked paths and is much more difficult to follow. We supply compass directions to help you through some of these turns, but if you find yourself feeling unsure about the route, simply retrace your steps and follow the railroad bed back out.

The focal point of this hike is locally prominent Bolton Notch. In general, a notch is a low spot in a mountain range, ridge, or other elevated hindrance to man's passage. The use of this particular dip in the ridge must certainly predate the early European settlers. The railroad blasted its way through here, and today an interstate highway (I-84) uses the same cut.

To start this hike you must approach the junction of US 6 and US 44A *from the east* on US 44A. Shortly before reaching the junction you pass a small shopping center on the left (at the traffic light) and then Mac's Lunch on the right. Park well off the road just beyond Mac's

Lunch and before the start of a guard rail.

Continue west, walking on the right-hand side of the highway, toward the notch; stay off the road as the traffic can be very heavy. Ignoring the passing automobiles, look for the sassafras, slippery elm, grapevines, poison ivy, Virginia creeper, and dewberry that grow along the roadside. The late summer field bouquet includes Queen Anne's lace, yellow evening primrose with its cross-shaped stigma, podded milkweed, burdock, black-eyed susans, thistles, tick trefoil, boneset, ripening pokeberry, and jewelweed. At this time, while the woods are still a uniform green, meadows are a riot of color.

Just past the large US 6 sign, follow a worn unmarked path diagonally right down a steep bank. At the bottom of the gully turn left. Pause a moment by the cement bridge abutment and look closely at the large silvery stone a foot or so to your right. The little brownish red nuggets in the stone are garnets, which are semiprecious stones when large and perfect. The rather soft silvery stone with embedded ultrahard garnets is found through this area of the state.

Now turn left along the cement abutment to reach the railroad bed where it emerges from the tunnel beneath the road system. We made a brief detour here to examine the tunnel and a little of the environs beyond.

The dirt railroad bed (the tracks were removed in 1976) is flanked by stone ramparts which were blasted out. In many places, the drill marks are plainly visible. The curved tunnel consists of a great arched roof and vertical sides—all cement. As you advance through the tunnel, the green vegetation becomes smaller and finally peters out. As you near the other side, the vegetation reappears: first patches of moss, then scraggly plants, and finally full growth.

Beyond the tunnel, the railroad bed lies between sheer twenty-foot-high rock walls. The right-hand wall is as fertile as the tunnel was bare. Dripping water maximizes the growth potential of this face. Mosses, more liverworts than you'd ever imagined possible, ferns, and grasses cover the rocks. The left-hand wall is more barren, but a few clumps of grass-of-parnassus make up for what it lacks in diversity. This lovely plant has rounded leaves and straight flower stalks crowned with creamy white blossoms whose petals are delicately etched with light green.

Retrace your steps through the tunnel and continue down the railroad bed. As long as you keep right where a dirt road touches the railroad bed, the next 2½ miles are straightforward. Along this stretch, we identified boneset, jewelweed, thistle, knapweed, primrose, blue curls (with prominent semicircular stamens), mullein, steeplebush, Joe-Pye weed, pepperbush, wild lettuce, various asters, green-flowered false nettle (no sting), Indian tobacco, and silverweed (our only white goldenrod). Many plants, especially the jewelweed, were cobwebbed with the parasitic leafless dodder, its small white flowers tucked close to its stem.

Numerous butterflies flitting along the cut seemed particularly attracted to the Joe-Pye weed. We saw fritillaries, black swallowtails, coppers, monarchs, and sulphurs.

While hiking this rich botanical area, especially near the road, try to avoid taking in the accumulation of broken bottles, discarded TV sets, and other detritus of our civilization. For obvious reasons sneakers are not recommended on the rough, broken, traprock surface of the railroad bed.

In 1½ miles, a roofed private picnic shelter appears on the right. When we first came to Connecticut almost twenty years ago, here, far from the nearest road, a two-story Victorian house was nestled against the railroad embankment. Sadly, it burned one winter in the mid-1960s.

In another mile, near a pile of railroad ties and an old road at left, take the worn unmarked path right (just before an old road cuts diagonally right). The route from here on is harder to follow. Go steeply down, with Valley Falls Pond glinting through the trees, to another worn path just above the water. Turn left, taking the wooden steps down to the edge of the pond.

Continue left along the pond and across the earthen dam decorated with several large willows to Valley Falls Park, run by the town of Vernon. The picnic shelter near the beach is handy on rainy days; for sunny days there are picnic tables along the pond's grassy edge.

Near the pond, we saw the deep purple flowers of New York ironweed, the yellow-centered blue flowers of the square-stemmed monkey flower, and the delicate white blossoms of the arrowhead. Many species of dragonflies and damselflies in various shades of blues, greens, and reds flitted over the pond. Several sectioned, gelatinous masses clung to a sunken branch: colonies of bryozoans or moss animals. Fewer than 50 of

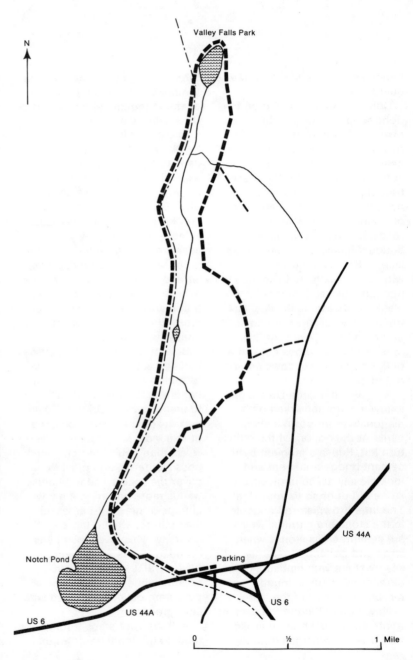

the more than 3,500 world-wide species of this animal are found in freshwater.

Continue beyond the shelter, cross the "frisbie" lawn, and pass through an aluminum gate just beyond a large, well-formed shagbark hickory. Unimpeded growth in an open area allows a tree to take the shape characteristic of the species.

For the next few hundred yards, the beaten path leads past overhanging grapevines and lush bushes of tartarian honeysuckle, barberry, and multiflora rose. In this avian Shangri-La, birds are heard and often glimpsed, but rarely observed. The fields which follow are most notable for Joe-Pye weed nearly nine feet tall.

After finally entering the woods on the old woods road with a grove of red pine at left, the trail jogs right at a fork through a small clearing. The curious purplish or chocolate-colored groundnut blossoms are entwined in the shrubbery here.

Soon a small stream trickles across the path. Bending left the trail climbs steadily past more red pines before crossing another seasonal trickle. In places, the path is deeply eroded by trail bikes. At a third grove of red pines, turn right downhill on the smaller path rather than left uphill on the more heavily worn way.

The trail is fairly well worn and should not be too hard to follow. After bearing to the right downhill for a while and passing another pair of seasonal trickles, it bends left (east) going steadily uphill. At a junction with another trail near the top of the hill go right (south) on the flat. You soon curve left uphill again. At the tote road near a red outbuilding, head right (southwest) gently down and at the next two forks bear left. Continue to bear left (south) until you reach the tote road a few yards beyond a stream (crossing on the left is easiest). Follow the tote road right (west); in less than ¼ mile it intersects a dirt road. Here you bear left again. A short distance beyond the bridge over the railroad bed, take the path left down the embankment to the bed. Turn right and retrace your steps to your car.

29 Westwoods

Total distance: 6 miles
Hiking time: 3½ hours/Rating: CD
Highlights: Rocks and ledges

This 2,000-acre, open space area in Guilford is an attractive woodland with a touch of salt. The lake at the far end is brackish and as you hike the labyrinth of trails, gulls wheel overhead. Westwoods is especially prized being so near Connecticut's overdeveloped coast.

From the junction of US 1 and CT 77 in Guilford proceed west on US 1 for .7 mile. When you reach Bishop's Apples on the right, turn left onto Peddler's Road. In 1 mile, turn left again on a rough dirt road into the woods. You arrive at an open recreation area in .2 mile where there is ample parking.

Westwoods, like Sleeping Giant (see Hike 42), has an extensive trail system. On the hike described here, follow the white circle trail out and the orange circle trail back. In the interest of clarity and brevity, we won't mention the numerous other trails you cross; directions to other routes in Westwoods are available in the *Connecticut Walk Book.* In general, however, the trails blazed with painted circles run north-south and those with painted squares, east-west. Mosquito repellent is a must on this hike in summer. Along the shore, because of extensive marshy breeding grounds, these

Brackish Lost Lake

pests always seem bigger, bolder, and more numerous than elsewhere.

The white circle trail starts on the left side of the recreation area entrance road, and shortly skirts a stone wall for a while before crossing it and heading downhill. In late May your way is strewn with the fallen white petals of flowering dogwood —nature's confetti.

Cross the Great Marsh plank walk slowly enough to appreciate the rich diversity of plants but quickly enough to avoid being eaten alive! At the start you see the sharply notched, paired, short-stemmed leaves of the arrowwood, the wedge-shaped leaves of the coastal pepperbush, the broad leaves of the skunk cabbage, and the large fronds of the cinnamon fern encircling its large cinnamon colored fertile fronds. Bunched tussocks of sedges ride the muddy area, the old dead leaves and roots forming the clump from which the new razor-sharp, grasslike leaves sprout.

Leaving the plank bridge at a junction—stay on the white circle trail—you rise into a dry, thin-soiled area covered with laurel and hemlock. In general, the trails flirt with a multitude of rocks, ledges, and rounded out-croppings; they were laid out with much thought and care. The

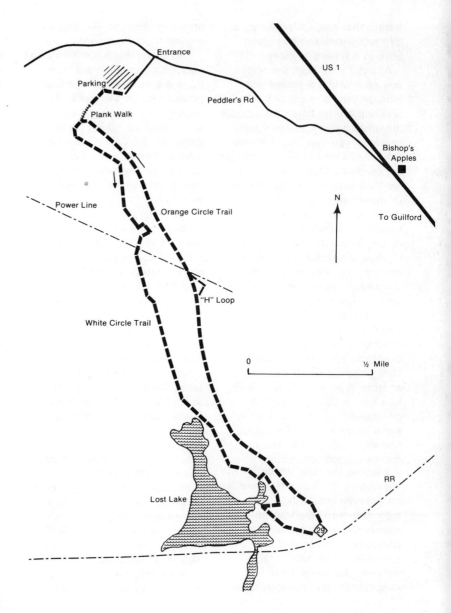

terrain that made Westwoods a farmer's wasteland has given birth to a hiker's wonderland!

About 1 mile from the start you pass under a power line. Pink ladyslippers grace the trailside and are scattered throughout the undergrowth. If you listen carefully you may pick out the szweet-szweet-chur-chur-chur of the cardinal. This striking bright red bird has become common in Connecticut only in the last few decades. The possible explanations of this expansion of its range, which include climatic change, extensive artificial winter feeding, and response to agricultural changes, provoke lively ornithological discussions.

After some 2 miles of walking you catch your first glimpse of brackish Lost Lake from a ledge overlook. You actually reach the phragmite-bordered shores in another ½ mile, and then climb to a final ledge which offers good views off the trail to the right. Since this spot is about halfway through the hike, it makes a good lunch stop.

Leaving the lake, watch for the old quarry on the right where the trail curves left. Broken slabs with drill-marked edges lie between it and the trail. Look carefully. You can pick out examples of stonecutters' whimsey here and there —scalloped rocks, hollowed-out boulders, and the like that were etched in idle moments.

You soon reach junction 29 at about 3 miles. All major junctions are numbered with signs placed high in the trees to avoid souvenir-hunting vandals, the worst kind for hiking trails. Keyed to the park's map, which may be found in the *Connecticut Walk Book,* these numbers enable you to place yourself exactly.

Turn sharply left onto the orange circle trail; shortly you pass through a hemlock grove so thick no undergrowth exists, a stark contrast to the lush woods you hiked through earlier. The combination of thick-foliaged branches and thick, dry, tannin-rich needles on the forest floor serves to exclude all plant life from the understory.

Be careful; shortly the trail takes a sharp right turn off the seemingly obvious downhill route, passes an overhang and clambers over loose rocks and ledges. The crevice to the right would be a poor place to wait out an earthquake!

Pursuing this route you come down by a very large overhang, the so-called Indian Caves. Turn right; the top dot in all Westwoods turns indicating double blazes is displaced in the direction the trail turns, a new, very helpful innovation in trail marking. Here you can either continue straight on the orange circle trail or turn right again onto the orange "H" trail. This side loop ascends a ledge on a sturdy ladder and makes a few rocky twists before rejoining the orange circle trail.

Bearing right, you soon pass beneath the power line again at about 5 miles. At about 5¾ miles the orange circle trail rejoins the white circle trail just before the plank walk. Cross the marsh and return to your car.

30 Bullet and High Ledges

Total distance: 6 miles
Hiking time: 3½ hours/Rating: C
Highlights: Views, interesting stream

Stone wall flanking the Narragansett Trail

People talk of the megalopolis extending from north of Boston to south of Washington, D.C., but there is a gap in this urban sprawl. This hike is in the middle of that precious open area. Even as we write, pressure groups, in the name of economics, are trying to run an interstate highway through the land. Hike here and judge the value of this area for yourself!

The Narragansett Trail to Bullet and High ledges leads west from CT 49, 4.8 miles south of Voluntown. Coming from Voluntown, pass Sand Hill Road on the left and then turn right on the second paved road. Park beyond the stop sign, opposite a formidably spined honey locust tree.

To pick up the blue blazes, walk a short distance down the pavement to a rutted dirt road on the left flanked by stone walls. (The paved road curves right to rejoin CT 49, .3 mile north of a striking white-steepled church. The eastern section of the Narragansett heads off here.)

On the right you pass a large sycamore with a massive poison ivy vine climbing one side. A thick mat of fibrous, aerial roots holds it in place. With clusters of three shiny leaves, this vine is easy to recognize in the summer, but you should become familiar with all its parts. The dormant winter vine is equally poisonous, especially when the sap courses up the stalks in preparation for spring growth.

The trail continues generally downhill. In .3 mile turn right off the dirt road, crossing a stone wall. Here the forest floor is thickly carpeted with club mosses: first ground cedar alone (many topped with candelabra-shaped spore stalks), then mixed with ground pine until finally the ground pine dominates. Past the club mosses, you find the rounded masses of gray green reindeer moss. The winter mainstay for caribou herds of the north, this "moss" is in fact a lichen.

The trail curves left by a clump of eight gray birches through a thick patch of greenbrier with black-tipped thorns. It then heads right along a seasonal stream and over a stone wall to Myron Kinney Brook, a river in microcosm. Nature's immutable laws are more easily observed when the familiar is seen in a different scale. Spring runoff forms the seasonal headwater of this small brook. Within a few tenths of a mile, small dendritic tributaries entering from both banks swell the brook many times. The water volume increases further from hidden springs where the stream cuts into the permanent water table.

Walk slowly along the stream with an alert eye; the forms darting across gravel riffles and deep pools are trout. Since native brook trout depend on a never-ending supply of ice-cold water, you see them in abundance only when you have passed the point where the brook has cut into the permanent water table.

While you are looking for trout, notice how the current rushes around the outside curves, undermining the banks. Sediment cut from these shores is carried downstream and deposited in sandbars on inside curves where the current is slower.

You leave the brook in ¼ mile and turn left uphill. The trail then dips to cross a small stream. Fleshy green ribbons cling with numerous, short, hairlike roots to the sphagnum moss along the banks. This is liverwort. An evergreen closely related to the mosses, it is one of the most primitive living plants.

Across the stream the trail hugs a stone wall up the hillside. With posted land on the right and state forest on the left, follow the blue blazes carefully through the network of interlocking tote roads and stone walls.

In an area of prominent ledges, the trail forks left. After

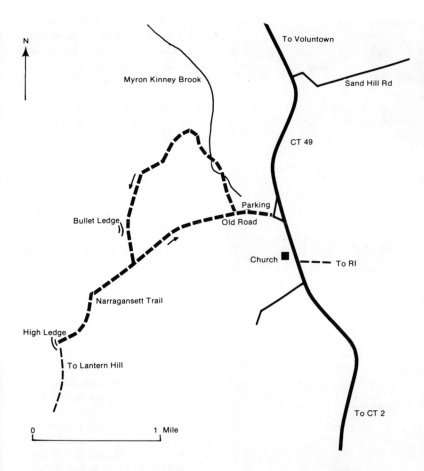

swamp, turn left. Following the blue blazes at succeeding junctions, you emerge finally on a deeply rutted old town road flanked by stone walls. To the left, this road leads back to CT 49.

Turn right instead for the climb to High Ledge. Fork left off the road by the trail sign that indicates it is .7 mile to the ledge and 7 miles to Lantern Hill (see Hike 40).

The trail climbs onto an oak and hemlock ridge. After about ½ mile it dips slightly into the valley before quickly rising to the edge of a steep hill. You pass through ledges just before dropping again into a narrow, rocky valley. Cross the stream and climb steeply, bearing left to High Ledge.

A rocky point perched above the valley, High Ledge affords a bird's eye view of nearby treetops. Island-dotted Wyassup Lake sparkles in the middle distance. The faint line of Long Island Sound can be seen beyond the lake against the horizon. On the right you can pick out the fire tower on Wyassup Lake Road.

If you wish to hike a full 7 miles, simply retrace your footsteps. The alternate route back along the rutted old town road to CT 49 shortens the distance by 1 mile.

¼ mile bear left again onto an old eroded road. The undulating footpath passes through cozy cornered stone walls and a partially cutover area with mountain laurel stalks as thick as a man's arm. When the trail drops steeply right, continue straight to the

Bullet Ledge lookout. Step carefully; copperheads are sometimes found here.

Return to the trail, descending to the rocky valley floor. When you reach the tote road set between a rock ridge and a

31 Natchaug

Total distance: 6.6 miles
Hiking time: 4 hours/Rating: CD
Highlights: Frog pond, great dead chestnut

Hulk of a giant chestnut

Many areas of Connecticut are losing trails because of development, disgruntled landowners, or other conflicting uses, but in eastern Connecticut, trails are expanding. The greatest growth has occurred around the University of Connecticut at Storrs on the Nipmuck and Natchaug Trails. The Nipmuck has been extended fourteen miles north to Bigelow Hollow State Park near the Massachusetts border (see Hike 22), while an eight-mile addition to the Natchaug now connects this newest of Connecticut's Blue Trails to the older Nipmuck to form a continuous trail nearly fifty-five miles long. This hike samples an interesting section of the Natchaug Trail.

From the junction of CT 198 and US 44 in Phoenixville, drive south on CT 198 for .5 mile. Turn left on General Lyons Road; in .1 mile turn right on Pilfershire Road and then right again in 1.7 miles on Kingsbury Road. In about 1 mile, this road becomes dirt. Shortly the blue-blazed Natchaug crosses, following a gravel way to Beaver Dam Brook Wildlife Marsh. Take this short feeder road left to the parking lot at its end.

The trail curves left, but the earthen dam of the pond to the right is worth the short detour. A granite and concrete apron handles the pond's spring overflow, but the summer stream slips down a vertical corrugated pipe which acts as a debris screen. The croak-jump-splash of thousands of frogs heralds your approach to the water's edge. The pond surface is almost completely covered with floating and emergent vegetation, especially the rather dull yellow-blossomed bullhead lily and the exotic white-flowered water lily. Tall emergent purple spires of pickerel weed line the shallow shoreline.

Return to the trail which parallels the pond. Several highbush blueberry bushes tempt you to dally and the perfume of the pepperbush lightens your way. In late summer the woodland birds are quiet; they anticipate the coming of fall sooner than we do. Swallows line the telephone wires (they are gone by Labor Day) and families of flickers and towhees rummage through the woods together. The hen grouse that diverted you from her chicks a month or two ago by feigning a broken wing is now just another member of the family group that flushes at your approach.

After passing through a grove of spruce, you reach Kingsbury Road again in about .6 mile; follow the road right. There are

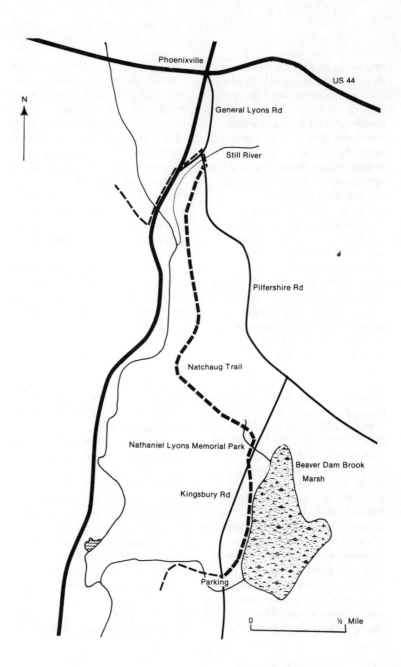

two kinds of safe three-leaved vines along here: the hog peanut, whose attractive lilac blossoms belie its name, and virgin's bower with its fragrant white blossoms. The orange flowers of the aptly named jewelweed, whose foliage is reputed to be a remedy for poison ivy, enliven the roadside greenery.

About .8 mile from the start the trail enters the woods on the left and soon passes through Nathaniel Lyons Memorial Park, named for the first Union general to die in the Civil War. The park features picnic tables, outhouses, a water pump, and a great stone fireplace. Midway across the open area bear left down an old tote road. On this stretch you wander through mixed hardwood forest, pass occasional stone walls, and invade the stillness of a hemlock grove.

In 1.9 miles, the erect hulk of a giant chestnut, 15½ feet around, commands your attention. It has been dead for nearly seventy years, and its seemingly indestructible wood is finally breaking down. In the last five years, most of its upper branches have fallen; the rot around the base is more obvious; and splits are showing here and there in the trunk. Except for a few black birches, the space around the patriarch is respectfully empty. The chestnut sprouts nearby are probably from the roots of the dead hulk.

While we were admiring this still-standing relic of our once most valuable hardwood, a small, chunky, brownish gray form circled a stub and disappeared into a knothole. This was only the second nocturnal flying squirrel we have seen in the woods. Its chunky look derives from the folds of skin joining the front and rear legs that allow this little creature to glide (not fly) from a high point.

A little farther along on the left, a much smaller dead chestnut also still stands. At 2.3 miles you come to a grouping of circular piles of stones, many on large embedded rocks. In the days of small hand tools like scythes, this was an efficient method for clearing fields—and quicker than building a wall; with today's straight-line mowing machines, it is unacceptable.

Checkered leaves of the rattlesnake plantain line the trail. Its faded spires of orchids thrust upward here and there. This has to be one of the few plants whose foliage is more familiar than its flowers.

In about 2.6 miles, turn left down a rutted road; the trail passes an area to the left where hemlocks were recently logged. Soon turn right into the woods and then bear right again at a wooded grassy remnant of field dotted with red cedars.

Dropping down a bank, you reach and follow the Still River, a trout stream, to the right. In the next .5 mile, you alternately pass through typical woodland and grassy woods featuring the short-lived American hornbeam, or musclewood, so-named because its corded appearance is similar to that of a muscular arm contorted with strain. For some reason it doesn't shade out grass, as do most trees.

After 3.3 miles you reach Pilfershire Road. Retrace your steps back over the trail—it looks different going the other way!

32 Peoples Forest

Total distance: 6¼ miles
Hiking time: 4 hours/Rating: C
Highlights: Views, secluded woods

Clintonia berries

Good hiking trails do not just happen nor are they maintained effortlessly. Three groups care for most of Connecticut's trails. The Connecticut Chapter of the Appalachian Mountain Club covers the Appalachian Trail, and because of the club's size and organization does an excellent job. The unpaid volunteers of the Connecticut Forest and Park Association maintain the extensive Blue Trail system. Because each trail section in this system is the domain of a single individual who is subject to the vagaries of time and temperament, occasionally a Blue Trail is slightly unkempt. But overall, these volunteers do a superlative job. By far the least maintained are the trails covered by the state. While some parks and forests have the money and personnel to keep their trails in tip-top shape, the Peoples State Forest is an example of an excellent trail system suffering from a lack of both. Don't miss this hike—it's a good one —but save it until you are sure of yourself in the woods. The trails need clearing and/or fresh paint, but with some care you should have little trouble following them.

From the junction of CT 318 and US 44 east of Winsted,

proceed east on CT 318 across
the Farmington River and take
the first left (East River Road). In
.8 mile, by the Peoples Forest
sign, fork right on the gated
paved state forest road (you
have missed the turn if you come
to the picnic area). Then, in
.2 mile, turn left up a short gravel
road to a parking area by a well-
built but now-vacant trailside
museum.

A trail, blazed in both orange
and blue, starts into the woods
here on your right. Follow this
path. Shortly the blue-blazed
Robert Ross Trail breaks off to
the left; stay on the orange-
blazed Agnes Bowen Trail as it
curves right through a white pine
grove to a tar road. In a few
yards the trail bears right off the
road by a forest "Trail" sign.
Almost immediately you cross a
small stream, which the now
rocky trail follows uphill to the
left. In ½ mile the trail passes
through a roadside picnic area
and in another 1 mile intersects
the yellow-blazed Charles Pack
Trail.

Turn right to follow the yellow
blazes. In a few yards you reach
Beaver Brook, which you cross
on a footbridge built by the
Youth Conservation Corps in
1976. On the right you can see
the old highwater double cable
crossing; you would walk on the
lower cable and use the upper

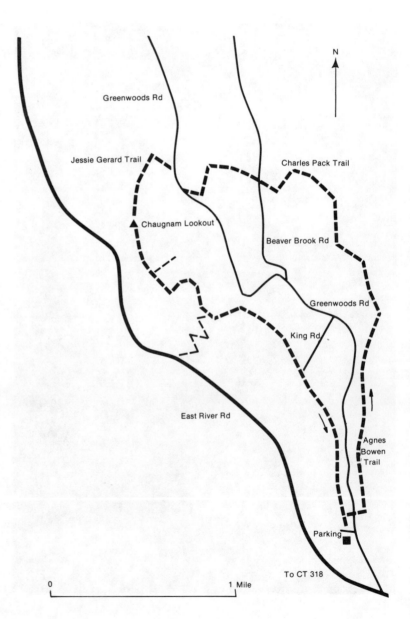

one for balance.

After crossing bear left across the hillside, keeping the beaver pond of Beaver Brook on your left, and then curve right uphill. One-half mile from the junction with the orange-blazed trail you cross a gravel forest road. You cross it again in another ½ mile and then drop downhill for ¼ mile to recross the brook on the Beaver Brook Road bridge. Watch for trout swimming in the crystal clear water. The trail reenters the woods on the stream's far side and shortly fords a small feeder brook. Another ¾ mile of woods walking brings you to Greenwoods Road, where this trail ends.

Step across the pavement and cut to the right through the picnic area to another "Trail" sign on your left. Here you pick up the Jessie Gerard Trail, which leads back toward your car. Note the poisonous, metallic blue clintonia berries beside the path here. Although found locally, this wide-leaved lily is more common in northern New England.

This trail, also blazed in yellow, traces an old tote road for a short distance before taking an obscure path uphill. After passing between two huge glacial boulders, the trail turns right toward Chaugham Lookout. These open ledges ½ mile from Greenwoods Road provide an excellent view across a wide, wild wooded valley. The canoe-dotted Farmington River winds sinuously below. The well-worn trail continues through hemlocks along the ledge escarpment.

Proceeding steeply down, you find sweet lowbush blueberries flanking the trail over erosion-bared bedrock. The yellow-blazed Jessie Gerard and blue-blazed Robert Ross trails run together here. The two split ¾ mile from Chaugham Lookout. (The yellow trail turns right and descends 299 steps to an old Indian settlement at a place called Barkhamstead Lighthouse.) Continuing on the blue-blazed trail another mile, you hit the terminus of gravel King Road. Turn right down the tote road that is marked at the start by a fence post and an orange blaze. Be careful here—the blue-blazed trail makes an obscure left turn in less than 100 yards where the tote road curves right.

Continue downhill on the blue trail, which joins the orange trail about 200 yards from the deserted museum. Follow the blazes to the right back to your car.

33 Mount Higby

Total distance: 5 miles
Hiking time: 3¼ hours/Rating: B
Highlights: Cliff views

This is the hike that ancient vulcanism built; Mount Higby is a traprock ridge. The rough footing is counterbalanced by sweeping views of woods, pastoral settings, or superhighways, depending upon where you look.

You start this hike at the junction of CT 66 and CT 147, west of Middletown. Park in the gravel lot well behind Guida's Drive-In. Walk east (inside the guard rail) on CT 66 for .2 mile, and then head right across the ditch and up into the woods on the blue-blazed Mattabesett Trail.

The small pine-tree-like plants you see along the paved road are horsetails, diminutive descendants of ancient forests. Eons ago they, along with club mosses and ferns, dominated the land, towering over one hundred feet high. The silification of their cells suggests their colonial use and name—scouring rush.

At first, the trail threads through hemlocks parallel to a tote road off to the right, but you soon begin to climb the cobbly traprock slopes. After several switchbacks, you finally come out of the stony woods at the Pinnacle, 1 mile from your start. Across CT 66 is Mount Beseck with Black Pond at its base. Continuing, you hike close

Looking north along the cliffs of Mt. Higby

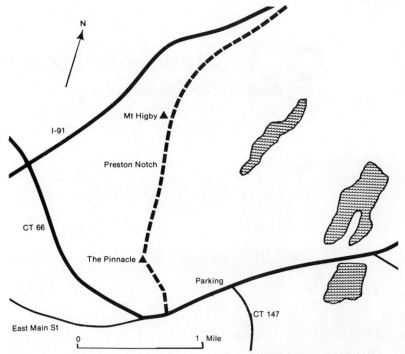

to the cliffs with excellent views in an unfolding panorama. West Peak and Castle Crag (see Hike 49) are visible in the middle distance; on the right is a traprock quarry; and the fields below provide excellent examples of nature's ever-ready invaders. In some the spirelike evergreen cedars are just springing up amid the pioneer weeds, in others cedars obscure the former pastures, and in still others the succeeding hardwoods are shading out the cedars. Forest succession silently continues.

At your feet you find large mats of creeping evergreen shrubs—bearberry. The white or pink bell-shaped flowers and tasteless seedy berries are borne in terminal clusters. The Indians smoked the foliage in a mixture with tobacco called kinnikinnik (reputed to be the longest single-word palindrome in the "English" language).

At 1.7 miles the trail drops down into Preston Notch and then climbs a cliff with additional superb views. Along this cliff look for a natural bridge formation with "N.B." painted on it. Scanning the horizon from the summit on a clear day, you see to the left Long Island Sound and the New Haven skyline. To its right is the long traprock dike traversed by the Regicides Trail (see Hike 50) and the lumpy mass of the Sleeping Giant (see

Hike 42). In front of you is an I-91 interchange; the large building on the right is the University of Connecticut Medical Center in Farmington.

This is also an excellent spot to review visually the northern Mattabesett and southern Metacomet Trails. Ahead at the end of the ridge you are hiking, the Mattabesett follows a tar road over I-91, enters the woods and climbs Chauncey Peak (see Hike 27) just left of the traprock quarry. It continues back along that ridge over Mount Lamentation (partially hidden from view) ending on the Berlin Turnpike (CT 5-CT 15).

The Metacomet picks up where the Mattabesett ends, heading west from the Berlin Turnpike over Castle Crag and West Peak (see Hike 49). It then proceeds north on the ridge past the Heublein Tower (see

Hike 34) and eventually reaches the Massachusetts border at Rising Corners.

From this cliff edge, the trail drops down and then climbs to another viewpoint. On a clear day you can see the Hartford skyline on the right with Mount Tom, north of Springfield, Massachusetts, to the east on the horizon. To the right of Mount Tom the Holyoke Range stretches like a roller coaster—the gap between the two is threaded by the Connecticut River. In the notch between the Holyokes and Mount Norwottuck on the far right there is a traprock quarry.

At this point take the time to review what you've seen and implant it firmly in your mind; with time these mountains will become old friends. Have lunch and enjoy the view you've earned. When rested, retrace your steps to the car.

34 Heublein Tower

Total distance: 7 miles
Hiking time: 4 hours/Rating: C
Highlights: Scenic reservoir, views, tower

Close by the city of Hartford is a large attractive open space area —reservoir land. Preserved to maintain water purity, areas such as this one in West Hartford are often open to nonpolluting activities. A nice day brings out an endless procession of casual walkers, joggers, bicyclists, hikers, and, in winter, ski tourers. The value of this land is incalculable.

From the junction of US 44 and CT 10 in Avon, proceed east on US 44 for 2.2 miles. On the left, a sign indicates Reservoir 6, Metropolitan District. Turn in here; there is ample parking.

Walk to the far end of the parking lot and bear left on the dirt road that is barred to motor vehicles. This becomes the blue-blazed Metacomet Trail. Along the way, the great rhubarblike leaves of the burdock abound; their nondescript flowers yield the round, multihooked burrs that dogs and hikers pick up in the fall. The fresh spring growth of grapevines edging out onto the road will be beaten back by the pounding feet of joggers. Shaded by hemlock, spruce, and pine, this west shore of Reservoir 6 is lovely any time of the year.

The wind-stirred wavelets on

Looking west from the escarpment

the reservoir reflect the sun as a sparkling glitter that gives life to the shifting scene. Along the shallow edges of the water numerous members of the sunfish family swim; this border area provides protection from predators and is handy to land-based insect life.

The small cement and stone bridge abutment at left is covered with great masses of poison ivy; in spring, nestled within its rash-inducing foliage are lovely greenish yellow blossoms. An unjaundiced eye sees beauty everywhere. Along here we saw a pair of black rat snakes, four feet long. Very effective rodent killers, they are now considered a threatened species by the Connecticut Herpetological Society.

Farther along, a great torrent is pouring into Reservoir 6, which is ducted from another reservoir in the system. Hartford gets most of its water from the Nepaug and Barkhamstead reservoirs in northern Connecticut; the West Hartford reservoirs serve largely for holding and storage rather than as prime sources of water.

Beyond this viewpoint, just before another culvert buttressed by stone and cement some 1½ miles from the start, turn left into the woods on an unmarked tote road by a pair of large oaks

springing from a single base.

For a while you parallel the reservoir. Watch out for rampaging chipmunks — they are numerous and active. At the fork bear left, following the path up a gentle grade. At the T junction,

go left again. At the next fork, just before the power line, bear left a third time and continue across erosion-bared traprock into the woods. Shortly you cross a pipeline clearing. About 50 yards beyond that, you reach yet another junction; turn left here and at the tote road junction farther on.

This lane leads a short distance up a steep grade to a low-use tar road about 3 miles from the start. Follow this road uphill to the right to the Heublein Tower, the fourth and most ornate observation tower situated on the ridge top. Built in 1914, this structure was home to the family of Gilbert Heublein, the liquor magnate, for over thirty years. On a clear day, the sharp-eyed can survey 1,200 square miles—on the horizon you can pick out New Hampshire's Mount Monadnock some eighty miles to the north, the Berkshires in western Massachusetts, the hills of eastern Rhode Island, and Long Island Sound to the south.

After enjoying the tower view, proceed south along the cliff escarpment through the picnic area and past a pavilion with a lovely view across the Farmington River valley. A couple of side paths lead to the right to cliff views limited by vegetation. Continuing on the escarpment path, you pass a small cedar gazebo. Just beyond, nearly ½ mile from the tower, bear left downhill to the tar road. Follow it left a few yards and then turn right into the woods on the trail you came up earlier.

Proceed downhill to the first fork and turn left. In ½ mile, you cross the power line. Continuing on this route past a tote road entering at left, you reach a hard-packed dirt road in ¼ mile —the blue-blazed Metacomet Trail. Turn right.

After crossing the pipeline you reach the fork at the head of the reservoir. Bear left to survey the east shore. As you top a hill, the Metropolitan District Commission's filtration plant for Bloomfield comes into view. Beyond it is the Hartford skyline. The dirt road joins and briefly follows a tar road along the wooded shore.

Keep to the dirt lane when the pavement bears away from the reservoir's edge. Looking back, you can see the Heublein Tower thrusting above the ridge. The rock riprap below you eliminates erosion of the reservoir banks.

When you come to a tar road again, stay on the path between it and the water. At the fork, bear left uphill away from the reservoir. (A right turn will take you out to the end of a point of land that is worth the detour.) After crossing a causeway, you soon emerge on the tar road within sight of the parking lot.

35 Bear Mountain

Total distance: 5.6 miles
Hiking time: 4 hours/Rating: B
Highlights: Connecticut's highest summit, views

Monument on Bear Mt.

A rugged, windswept mountain with views into three states awaits you at the high point of this hike. On the way, you hike a portion of the famous Appalachian Trail (AT). The top of Bear Mountain boasts a magnificent stone monument that proclaims —incorrectly—this to be the highest point in Connecticut; in fact, as has been discovered since World War II, the high point is on a shoulder of nearby Mount Frissell, whose summit lies in Massachusetts.

To reach this hike's start, drive on CT 41 north 3.2 miles from its junction with US 44 in Salisbury. There is a small hiker's parking lot on the left. (During the spring thaw, the mud here may be hubcap deep.)

The Under Mountain Trail— a feeder to the AT—starts a few yards north of the lot where there are blue blazes on a tree and the adjacent stone wall. Proceed through the wall into a flat field that is rapidly becoming overgrown. Enter the woods and start to climb, gently at first, then more steeply. This trail presents an almost unrelieved steady climb for 2 miles. It is a good test of wind and muscle and an excellent place to practice a mile-eating trick used by seasoned hikers: set a pace you can maintain all the way to the top without stopping.

After ¼ mile, you pass an eroded gully at right and the hulks of several large fallen chestnut trees at left. Although these trees have been dead for at least sixty years, their trunks still litter the forest floor. The bark-less, solid remains have a special weatherbeaten look no other dead tree has.

As you climb, it becomes more obvious that the trail is an old tote road whose surface has eroded several feet into the hill. Soon you encounter a bad wash-out. This unsightly scar was caused by hikers! The constant trampling of feet killed the stabil-izing vegetation, and the deeply eroded road did not permit the diversion of water off the trail. Then a real gully-washer of a storm, probably in the spring when soil is already saturated and unstable, caused the muddy earth to slide into the ravine on the left, leaving the gouge in the trail you see before you. Since the water runoff now flows into the ravine, the base of the wash-out should be fairly secure.

If you are hiking when the leaves are off, you will glimpse the Twin Lakes to your right. During the last ½ mile or so, you cross several small streams; one near the top of this feeder trail has a year-round flow.

After 2 miles, you emerge on the white-blazed AT. Observe this junction carefully as you also come back this way and wouldn't want to miss your turn —the AT south goes all the way to Georgia!

The Blue Trails may be under-used, but this famous trail is definitely overused. If you want to avoid your fellow man, this is not the path to hike. Follow the AT right, and at the first fork bear right again. Your route, made uneven by eroded rock and protruding ends of ledges, continues its gradual but steady climb to the summit of Bear Mountain, .8 mile from the feeder trail. The small oaks become more stunted, stubby bear oaks mix in and then dominate, and picturesque scrub or pitch pines dot the upper slope.

The pines are worth a closer look. All lean east, away from the prevailing west winds. With patience that would shame a bonsai artist, the cold, dessicat-ing winds have carved off up-ward growth so that the tops are flattened and stream eastward.

Walk out on the first ledge to your right and look around. The whole area in view is known as the Riga Plateau; many small peaks rise out of the vast, wooded, rolling plateau. The peak at left which drops into the valley is Lion Head. To its left,

away from the plateau on the horizon, is Mohawk Mountain (see Hike 37), easily identified by its ski slopes and towers. In the middle distance, left of Mohawk, is Prospect Mountain with open fields on top. Almost directly behind you, on the plateau, is the rocky side of Gridley Mountain.

Return to the trail and con-tinue upward. Erosion has less effect here as much of the tread-way is on ledges. You soon reach a short worn path to a protruding ledge. From this rock Gridley Mountain (2,211 feet) to the west appears even sharper. To Gridley's right is Mount Frissell (2,453 feet) with Round Mountain (2,296 feet) directly in front of it. Right of Frissell is Ashley Mountain (2,390 feet). Gridley and Round are in Con-necticut while Ashley and Frissell are in Massachusetts.

As you rise on Bear Mountain, the Twin Lakes become more and more visible. East Twin is well known for its stocked kokanee salmon. Behind the lakes is the large hulk of Canaan Mountain.

Soon you reach the impres-sive, cement-capped stone monument on the summit of Bear Mountain (2,316 feet). The stone was engraved when it was believed that this was the highest point in Connecticut.

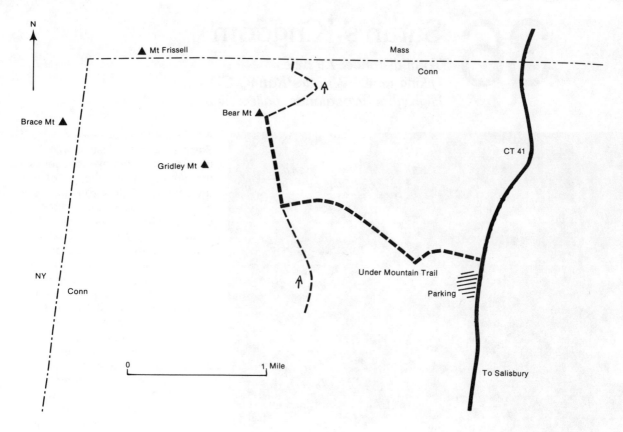

N

Mt Frissell ▲   Mass

Conn

Brace Mt ▲

Bear Mt ▲

CT 41

Gridley Mt ▲

NY

Conn

Under Mountain Trail

Parking

0   1 Mile

To Salisbury

While strolling around the open top, watch for large black soaring birds—turkey vultures. These birds, with a six-foot wingspan the largest of North America's vultures, are common in the adjacent Hudson River valley and are spreading throughout the northeast. They use rising columns of air along the edge of the Riga Plateau to soar for hours without flapping their wings.

From here the view south is hidden but it is what you have admired on the way to the top. To the east lie the Twin Lakes and Canaan Mountain. For the best view to the north, follow the AT to a ledge on the fringe of the scrub pines. The high mountain with the tower is Mount Everett (2,602 feet), the second highest mountain mass in Massachusetts. The hulk in front of it is Race Mountain (2,365 feet), a favorite of isolationists as a long hike on the AT from either direction is required to reach it. For the west vista proceed through a small pine-filled hollow onto the ledges beyond. From the right the mountains are Ashley, Frissell, Round (in front of Frissell), Brace (2,311 feet), South Brace (2,304 feet)—these last two are in New York—and Gridley. The body of water to the left of Gridley is South Pond (1,715 feet), and the mountains in the distance across the Hudson River valley are the Catskills.

It takes several visits before these mountains become old friends, but the journeys are definitely worth the effort! As we sit at home, we can picture this area in our mind's eye. When you can do that, its beauty is yours forever.

As you retrace your steps, continue to soak up the views from the open ledges. Be careful to go left at the junction with Under Mountain Trail.

36 Satan's Kingdom

Total distance: 7.9 miles
Hiking time: 4½ hours/Rating: CD
Highlights: Woodlands, valley view

A hike is a time for looking. Fresh air and exercise supplement the questing eye that seeks the rare or unusual aspects of the common. Below you club mosses send up spore stalks; the checkerberry sprouts tender young leaves; and the dodder's leafless, yellow, parasitic stems twine relentlessly on reluctant supporting vegetation. At eye level you notice the quantities of chestnut sprouts and the shad-bush leaves, wrinkled by blight. Above you the thick foliage of the hemlock and the graceful fine needles of the white pine catch the sun's rays, dimming the trail.

Watch for these and other things while you walk the Tunxis Trail. This section traces out a route through an area known as Satan's Kingdom. Many of the names used here date back to the state's early years.

From the junction of CT 179 and US 202 in Canton, follow US 202 west 2.5 miles to the blue oval "Tunxis Trail" sign. There is ample parking in a large pullout area .1 mile east of this sign. You may either walk back to the trail head or climb the short, steep slope from the parking area to the old road on which the trail starts.

Shortly, the blue-blazed trail

Fungi working on a dead tree

Tipping Rock ▲

Tunxis Trail

US 44

Farmington River

Rome Spare Outlook ●

Satan's Kingdom Rd

US 202

CT 179

Pine Hill Rd

N

0   1 Mile

enters the woods on the left and proceeds gently uphill. In .5 mile it joins an old tote road. Bear left and 1 mile from the start you reach Pine Hill Road. Turn right and then immediately left into the woods at the intersection with Tipping Rock Loop (no sign). You soon cross under a power line. In this area, the trail crosses and runs briefly with many woods roads; follow the blue blazes very carefully.

Soon after crossing a swamp-bottomed draw, you come to a trail junction by a great lichen- and fern-bedecked ledge, 2.3 miles from the start. Signs give directions and distances for the intersecting trails. Bear left on the Rome Spare Outlook Trail, named for one of Connecticut's early trail builders. Don't be confused by the Route 25 designations; these signs were put up before Route 25 was renumbered US 202.

In .1 mile you traverse the long, narrow Queen Mary Ledge. Be careful here in wet weather; the rocks are covered with lichens and may be slippery. Soon you pass three great white oaks. The first is a freshly fallen ruin; white fungal masses interlard the rotten heartwood. The second still stands, but its hollow center and top-heavy shape number its days. The third oak, while not quite as grand as the

other two, has a more compact form which should better withstand the rigors of time. It may still be standing when we and the other two oaks are but piles of dust.

One mile from the Rome Spare Outlook sign, you come to a flat with particularly black soil encircled by a ditch. A sign says "Charcoal Kiln." Roving woodsmen would cut hardwoods, pile the logs in a circle, cover them with earth, and let them burn with a minimum of air. The wood volatiles would distill off, leaving charcoal, which was then sold to iron smelters and others who needed hot, intense fires.

In another .2 mile (3.4 miles from the start), the trail ends in a small circle at the Rome Spare Outlook. After absorbing the views of the wooded valley, scattered fields, and farm buildings on the opposite hill, retrace your steps for 1.2 miles to the signed

trail junction.

Bear left onto the Tipping Rock Loop again. Shortly you arrive at Tipping Rock Ledge. One of the glacial erratics here used to be so poised that it would rock back and forth at the pressure of a hand. One day someone rocked it too hard, and it fell off its fulcrum—so much for nature's more fragile wonders.

The trail continues down the side of the ledge, joins a badly eroded motorcycle trail, and ends on dirt Satan's Kingdom Road .8 mile from the signed junction (5.5 miles from the start).

Go right on the road 1.4 miles to the junction with Pine Hill Road. Here jog right and then almost immediately left into the woods. You are now on the trail you followed in. Retrace your steps for 1 mile to your car.

37 Mohawk Mountain

Total distance: 6.4 miles
Hiking time: 4 hours/Rating: CB
Highlights: Views, spring

Mohawk Mountain (1,683 feet) rises above its surroundings offering a 360-degree view from its summit tower. This combination of state park and state forest provides many services: extensive picnic areas, water pumps, outhouses, roadside lookouts, lean-tos, a youth camping area, and ski slopes. Mohawk is fortunate in having parts of both the Appalachian Trail (AT) and the Mattatuck Trail (part of the Blue Trail system) within its boundaries. The trails, coming from divergent directions, meet near the summit and provide delightful alternatives to the summit road.

The entrance to Mohawk State Forest is on the south side of CT 4 exactly 4 miles west of the junction of CT 4 and CT 63 in Goshen. There is a parking area at the entrance. Dirt and tar roads with inviting picnic areas and scenic lookouts lace the forest.

Walk through the gate on the right and then turn left off the tar road onto a gravel one. Upon meeting the white-blazed AT, turn right into the woods. (A left turn takes you to Dean Ravine [see Hike 23] about ten miles away.) In a few yards, you pass a three-sided, Adirondack-type lean-to.

Stone tower on the Mattatuck Trail

The trail then dips into a wet area before passing a large protruding ledge with mosses, lichens, and ferns decorating its face and trees teetering on its rim.

Continue up the rocky slope onto the first of two rather flat terraces. Oaks, maples, birches, and black cherries shade the understory of laurel here. Close to the ground, mayflowers abound — we saw twelve patches in the first flat stretch. The delicate, fragrant, waxy blossoms of this low-growing trailing shrub have been its undoing. Picking wildflowers is a selfish habit at best, and it has been a major factor in the demise of this once common symbol of the Pilgrims. Bend low, sample their fragrance, admire their beauty, and leave them for the next person to enjoy.

The trail climbs to the second flat area with drier oak-dominated woods, descends to a grove of red pine, and then moves along and over a side hill. Follow down the hill, passing another lean-to at about 1.2 miles. You go through a stand of white birch and cross paved Toumey Road.

Across the road, a scenic turnout offers a view across the valley. The large mass to the right is the Riga Plateau; the higher peaks are, from the right, Everett (with the tower), Race,

and Bear (see Hike 35). To the left are the Catskills in New York.

Head left up the tar road; in 50 yards turn right into a red pine grove. Mixed in with the pine is the largest stand of striped, or goosefoot, maple we know of in Connecticut. Common in northern New England, it is found only at higher elevations in this state. The handsome green bark with vertical, broken white stripes and the large, goose-foot-shaped leaves explain its common names. Up north this short-lived, scraggly understory tree is also called moosewood, as that ungulate browses on its branches in winter and eats its leaves in summer.

The trail joins an old tote road and emerges by the chairlift at the top of the Mohawk Mountain Ski Area. Across the slope at the Pinnacle, there is a stone lookout tower.

The blue-blazed Mattatuck Trail starts at the tower. The AT and the Mattatuck run together briefly before the AT splits right .6 mile from the second lean-to. You keep left with the Mattatuck, which soon comes out at a picnic area on Mattatuck Road, the auto route to the summit.

Follow the road to the right a short way before turning right into another red pine grove. The pile of ruffed grouse feathers we

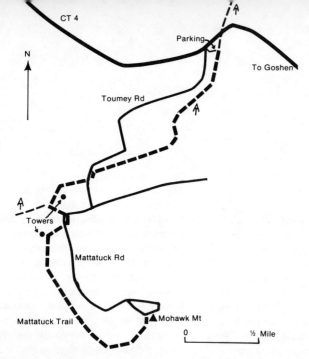

CT 4

N

Parking

To Goshen

Toumey Rd

Towers

Mattatuck Rd

Mattatuck Trail

▲ Mohawk Mt

0   ½ Mile

found here were probably pluck-
ings from the kill of a great
horned owl. A mouthful of
feathers is no more appealing to
him than it is to us.

The trail curves up onto
extensive flat ledges about
.4 mile from the AT-Mattatuck
split. The ruins of a great stone
tower dominate this rocky
stretch. Most of Connecticut's
forest stonework was done by
the CCC in the late 1930s; but
this steel-braced tower with its
magnificent fireplace was built
by a Seymour Cunningham in
1915; more than that we do not
know.

Now the trail drops again;
watch for an operating hand
pump in a little clearing. Since
this water is a little rusty, save
your thirst for the piped spring
coming up soon. Beyond the
clearing you pass through a
swampy area with several large
bull pines. The trail here may be
a little obscure. Bear slightly

right and follow the blazes
carefully.

On the far side of the swamp
you cross a stone wall and
follow left beside it. The trail
recrosses the wall by the piped
spring; a small cement cistern
protects the source. A friend of
ours claims a hiker should never
pass a spring without drinking,
even if only a sip—a symbolic
thanks for the water, the trail, the
day, and the good fortune to be
there.

Angle back toward the wall
and pass another lean-to on your
right about .5 mile from the
stone tower. The trail is stepped
up the slope ahead on embedded logs and rocks. Near the top
you clamber over boulders.
Across the valley, Mohawk's
summit towers are visible
through leafless trees. The trail
describes a great circle to your
left until it heads straight for
Mohawk. It levels, crosses a tote
road, and then rises through

laurel thickets to the gravel
summit road.

Head left up the road to the
top of Mohawk Mountain. There,
dwarfed by radio towers, a lookout tower rises just high enough
to top the trees. There are picnicking facilities and a parking
lot for the non-ambulatory who
arrive by auto on the gravel road.

Climb the steep wooden
tower steps and enjoy the
360-degree view. Again Mounts
Everett, Race, and Bear punc-
tuate the Riga Plateau to the
north. The Catskills rise on the
western horizon. Farther left, in
the distance, is the mountainous
area near Harriman Park in New
York. The large flat-topped mass
in the middle distance to the
right of the Riga Plateau is
Canaan Mountain. If your eye-
sight and the visibility are good
you should be able to pick out
Mount Tom in Massachusetts
some forty miles away. It lies
about thirty degrees right of
Riga, a distinctive blue outline
protruding above the horizon
with a gentle rise at left and a
steep cliff on the other side.

When your eyes have drunk
their fill, you can choose to
follow either the trail (3.2 miles)
or Mattatuck Road to Toumey
Road (a left turn) back to your
car. Although the trail is longer
than the road, it is easier on your
feet.

38 Mansfield Hollow

Total distance: 8 miles
Hiking time: 4½ hours/Rating: CD
Highlights: River walk, view

Shinleaf in flower

Because of its proximity to the University of Connecticut at Storrs, the Mansfield Hollow Dam Recreation Area is sprinkled with temporary refugees from academia: jogging professors, strolling students, and young families with toddlers. In addition to picnic tables, fireplaces, ball fields, bridle paths, rest rooms, and boat launching facilities, Mansfield Hollow also encompasses one of the two southern termini of the Nipmuck Trail, which stretches thirty-four miles north to Bigelow Hollow State Park near the Massachusetts border. This hike follows the Nipmuck through a flood control area and rolling countryside as far as "50 Foot," a nice little lookout.

From the junction of CT 89 and CT 195 in Mansfield Center, drive south on CT 195 for .5 mile to Bassetts Bridge Road and turn left. After .8 mile park in the lot on the right side of the entrance road to Mansfield Hollow Dam Recreation Area fields.

To reach the start of the Nipmuck Trail, follow the gravel entrance road through open fields to the pine-fringed woods, where a flood control causeway on the left leads to a second gravel road. Turning right, you soon find the Nipmuck's blue blazes leading into the pine woods on the left.

The trail starts on sandy soil, where the white pines grow well. You reach a tote road in .1 mile; the blazes lead to the right before turning left into the woods again. (You can see the flood control reservoir at the end of the tote road.) On your right are patches of shinleaf, which you can distinguish by their almost round evergreen leaves. Although you don't see their spikes of nodding white flowers until June and July, the flower buds may be found nestled beneath forest detritus in early May. This plant derives its name from the early custom of applying the leaves to sores and bruises—any plaster, no matter where applied, was called a shinplaster.

As you wend your way up onto a flat, the trail touches and then heads left off a bridle path. You flirt with numerous bridle paths strewn with strawberry plants and cinquefoils throughout the first part of this hike. The mixture gives you a chance to distinguish between these two plants with similar leaves: the strawberry has three-leaved bunches; the local cinquefoils, five.

Beneath a blue-blazed white pine you find the first of many hawthorns along the trail. This shrub is characterized by for-

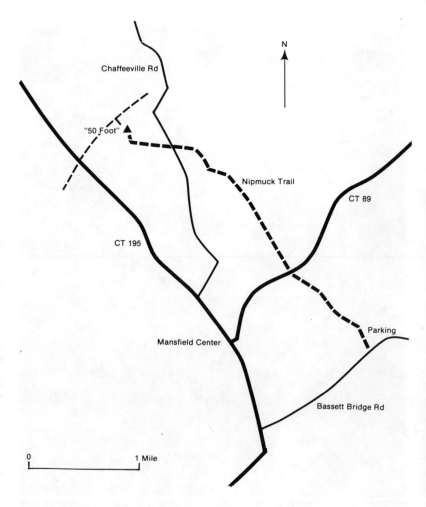

midable two-inch thorns, attractive white flowers with a rather disagreeable odor, and fall pomes suitable for jellies. You encounter and cross a second bridle path, pass through a third wooded section, and emerge once again on a bridle path.

At this junction, head right. After curving left through a small patch of woods, the trail continues along the right side of a ball field on a gravel road to CT 89, 1.5 miles from the start; follow the tar road briefly and then cross to a grassy area. Bear right down the hill by an old well and cellar hole; then proceed left on an abandoned tar road until the blazes head back into the woods on the right.

The trail now runs along the top of a dry dike. In flood times the central gates can be closed to limit downstream flooding. Several such dikes describe the flood control area.

At the far end of the dike turn right into the woods. White oaks (the bark is actually light gray) stand sentinel on the trail. When you come onto a gravel road, turn left.

A pair of telephone poles braced with steel beams carries the trail across the Fenton River. Often a phoebe nests under here —these birds favor various cosy "undersides" above a stream for nesting. Turn left by a dead elm

along the alder- and willow-lined river and then go right at a grassy fork. Blue blazes and painted wooden arrows guide you through this stretch. Robins run ahead of you in the grass and the soulful cry of the mourning dove echoes around you.

The path now angles up onto a gravel ridge deposited by a glacier, with the river below at left. To the left a small stream widens into swamp pools liberally populated with frogs and painted turtles.

Dropping off the ridge, you continue through a meadow brilliant with the bright yellows of the goldfinch and the swallowtail butterfly. Turn left into the woods just before you reach a second gravel ridge.

Shortly you come to the Fenton River again, which another pair of telephone poles bridges. After crossing, follow this thirty-foot-wide trout river upstream (right), keeping a cornfield on your left. The trail winds among worn fishermen's paths along the bank—watch the blazes carefully to avoid straying. Moisture-loving ferns grace the low spots, while the aptly named interrupted ferns stand tall throughout.

Two miles from CT 89 the trail cuts to the left away from the river and uphill to Chaffeeville Road. The trail crosses the road and rolls through hardwoods and

hemlocks. After crossing two small streams, it climbs steeply and then slabs a hillside. Columbine hangs from the dripping wet rock cliffs on the left.

Beyond drier cliffs higher up and just before a steep descent, leave the Nipmuck for an unmarked side trail through a cleft in the cliffs. You wind left past boulders and, less than ½ mile from Chaffeeville Road, emerge on top of a cliff. Known locally as "50 Foot," this lookout offers fine views of eastern Connecticut.

Enjoy your "lunch with a view," and then retrace your steps to your car.

39 Windsor Locks Canal

Total distance: 9 miles
Hiking time: 4½ hours/Rating: D
Highlights: Historic canal, riverside vegetation, wildlife

By the mid-nineteenth century stiff competition from railroads had combined with a shortage of bulk materials and an uncompromising terrain to bring about the collapse of New England's expanding canal system. The Windsor Locks Canal, built in 1829 to bypass the Enfield rapids on the Connecticut River, was an exception. Here the canal survived because water diverted from New England's largest river not only served barge traffic but also provided power to several mills, the last of which continued to operate until the 1930s. Today the Windsor Locks Canal still routes an occasional pleasure craft around the rapids, and its old towpath, now paved, offers a pleasant, level trail for walking or bicycling.

To reach the towpath, follow CT 159 south from its southern junction with CT 190 for .1 mile to Canal Road, on the left. The road ends in about .4 mile with a large parking lot. The lot is not indicative of trail use; it is used by fishermen who congregate here from April to June. The famous Enfield rapids provide the best ocean-run, shad-fishing site in New England.

Head south down river and pass through the gates to the

A young woodchuck along the towpath

start of the towpath. Your route simply follows the paved way 4½ miles to its end; there are no side trails to mislead you. The towpath is a designated bicycle trail, so please give cyclists the right of way.

While the plants and wildlife scattered along the way are the chief attractions of this hike, man-made constructions along the canal are not without interest. About 2 miles from the start, the blunt prow of heavily wooded, mile-long Kings Island comes into view. Notice here that the banks of the canal are formed of soft Connecticut Valley red sandstone. About 1/3 mile along Kings Island, you cross a small overflow dam built to handle flood waters from Strong Brook; smaller streams run directly into the canal. About ¼ mile below Kings Island, you pass alongside venerable stone abutments supporting a trestle over the Connecticut River; several trains whistled by as we hiked the towpath.

As you walk, maintain an alert eye. This entire strip is a veritable oasis in an urban desert. While we create monotonous sameness and crowd out sensitive lives, nature in her toughness moves in wherever possible.

We came upon a young woodchuck caught between the devil (us) and the deep blue sea (the

canal). Butterflies were constant companions. Beside that too common pest, the cabbage white, we saw swallowtails, skippers, wood satyrs, and a beloved ally, the red admiral, whose caterpillar is raised on nettles.

From a botanical point of view, this walk is one of the best in the state. We identified ox-eyed daisies, fleabane, yarrow, vetch, two varieties of milkweed, campion, St. Johnswort, black-eyed susans, goldenrod, mullein, deadly nightshade, thimbleweed, deptford pinks, plantains, roses, both bull and Canada thistles, gill-over-the-ground, jewelweed, day lilies, and lovely sundrops like giant buttercups with cross-shaped stigmas. The clovers, legumes with built-in nitrogen factories on their roots, are well represented. In addition to white alsike clovers we found at least two varieties of yellow-blossomed hop clovers.

Vines and bushes are everywhere: poison ivy, several varieties of grapes, Virginia creeper, sweet-smelling Japanese honeysuckle, scrub willow, various types of smaller dogwoods, elderberries, alder, sassafras, juniper, slippery elm, and sumac with great spires of red-ripening acid fruit.

Here also, trees that you usually see only from below on woodland trails stand open for your

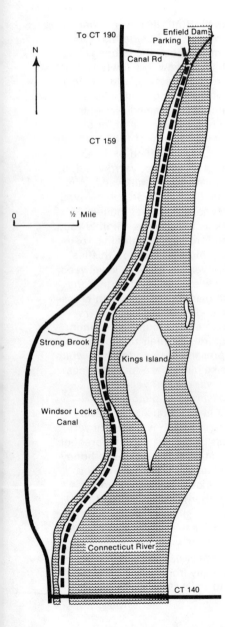

scrutiny. These trees growing on the river bottom or steep canal-side to your left present their seldom seen tops for your curiosity. The round buttons that give the sycamore one of its common names (buttonwood) are here at eye level and the stickiness of the butternut tree's immature nuts can be tested in place. In early summer you can pick with ease the tasty fruit of the red mulberry—if you can beat the birds.

We talk of waste areas, but probably the only true wastelands are those areas sealed with asphalt and concrete—and even these are transitory. A constant rain of seeds awaits the slightest moistened crack, ready to sprout and grow. Near the end of the towpath, we found that field bindweed had wrestled a foothold in the junction of an old brick building and the asphalt drive. In the wild the small white, morning-glory-like flowers of this weed may have little appeal, but here they enlivened a dingy corner.

A second set of gates 4½ miles from the first marks the end of the towpath near CT 140. Turn around and retrace your steps to the car.

40 Pequot Trail and Lantern Hill

Total distance: 8½ miles
Hiking time: 4¾ hours/Rating: CD
Highlights: Indian cemetery, views

Along the trail

Walk softly on this land once dominated by the mighty Pequot tribe. This hike starts by their burial ground, cuts through their reservation, and then climbs Lantern Hill, the legendary wartime lookout of Sassacus, the Pequot sachem. The flattish terrain typical of southeastern Connecticut makes the Pequot Trail hike a good one for families who wish to stretch beyond the usual five to six miles. If you wish a shorter hike, the 8.4 miles can be halved by leaving a second car at the Narragansett Trail crossing on Wintechog Hill Road off CT 2.

To reach the burial ground at the start, follow Shewville Road —a left turn about .2 mile west of the junction of CT 164 and CT 2 in Ledyard—south for 1 mile to Fanning Road. Turn right (west) and continue to a parking area on the left. (The paved surface becomes gravel after .4 mile.)

The blue blazes that mark the Pequot Trail pass through the parking area, but before you set out for Lantern Hill, walk up the dirt road that lies straight ahead. On an open, airy knoll left of a cedar post stockade you find Mashantucket, the largest known Pequot burying ground. Only remnant slabs of rock mark most of the graves, although the inscriptions can be deciphered on a few very recent headstones.

Retrace your steps to the parking lot and follow the blazes left into the woods. The trail slabs across the hillside. Watch here for dogwood trees—in both numbers and size, this area is one of the best in Connecticut.

The trail swings behind some houses, passes through a swampy area, and emerges on Shewville Road in about 1 mile. Head to the right, uphill on the road, for ¼ mile. At the crest, the trail enters the woods, left, and climbs steeply. Stop at the lookout near the summit of this hill. Except for a hilltop farm and a few smaller houses, the panorama north is of completely treed valleys and rolling hills. This is truly the "Megalopian Gap," the only break in the urban sprawl that stretches from Boston to Washington, D.C. Even now the highway lobby is trying to extend I-84 east from Hartford into this pristine area. Developers abhor open spaces.

The trail slopes gradually off the oak-covered hill, joins a tote road, and enters a partially cut-over area. Please stay on the trail; you are now on land that is part of the Pequot Reservation.

Unlike their western counterparts, most eastern Indians were reduced to reservation living three hundred years ago. Even earlier, epidemics of measles, smallpox, and other diseases brought in by European sailors and fur traders swept away whole tribes in southern New England. In the late sixteenth century the Mahicans (corrupted to Mohegans by the colonists) of the western New York Iroquois, 700 warriors strong, moved in and easily dominated the decimated tribes of Connecticut. Their unrelenting savagery earned them the name Pequot, a derivation from the Algonquin word meaning 'destroyer'. Friction with the Narragansetts to the east and the Bay Colony to the north plus the defection of Chief Uncas and his followers in the early 1630s culminated in the Pequot War of 1637, the first of America's Indian wars. The Pequots were slaughtered and the survivors enslaved on many colonial homesteads. Finally, in 1667, Connecticut assigned the tribe a permanent 220-acre reservation, which is still occupied by descendants of the original tribesmen.

Leaving the Pequot's land, the trail crosses several small streams and passes through groves of hemlocks and pines. At the fork, follow the blue arrow left. The trail soon enters an impressive rhododendron swamp and winds almost ¼ mile through this stand of large-leaved evergreens. The beautiful white flower sprays emerge around the first of July. The deep shade beneath the rhododendron dampens any extreme temperature fluctuations; the coolness that results in turn helps maintain these shrubs.

The trail rises from the swamp through hemlocks to a white pine grove. Follow the tote road up along the ridge to the left. Near the top of a hill an old stone wall encloses another cemetery. As in many small country cemeteries, one or two family names dominate—here it is the "Main" family.

Continue on the tote road to CT 214 (Indiantown Road); follow the pavement left to Lantern Hill Road. Turn right and shortly enter the woods on the left (watch carefully for the blazes). Because of the prevalence of hard-to-mark small brush, this ½-mile section of trail is poorly marked. After crossing a brook, bear left. Shortly head right on an old tote road past a cellar hole on the right. The footpath leaves the road, left, and gradually climbs a low ridge. The Pequot Trail ends at the junction with the Narragansett Trail. (A left takes you to Wintechog Hill Road in just under ¼ mile. There is ample parking on CT 2, just east of Wintechog Hill Road at the Lantern Hill parking lot.)

If the day is nice, head right on the Narragansett Trail. A fairly

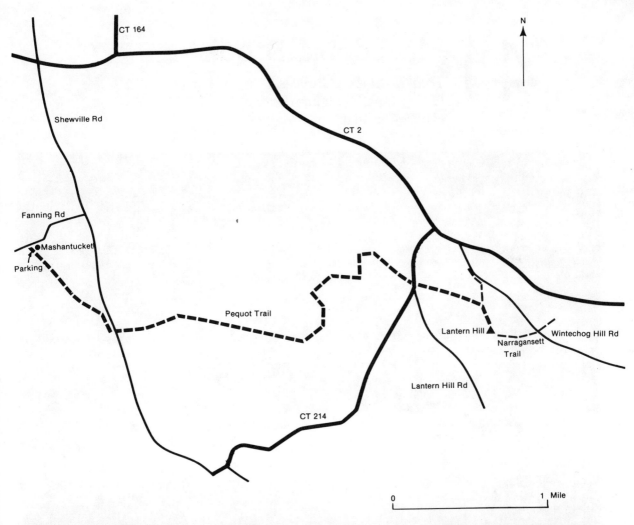

steep climb takes you to the summit of Lantern Hill in just over ¼ mile.

At least three different stories are associated with the origin of the name "Lantern Hill." One says that the summit was used by the Pequot sachem Sassacus as a lookout during the 1637 Pequot War, the second that the sun shining on the white quartz crystals created a "lantern" to the guide sailors at sea, and the third that a watch was maintained here during the War of 1812 with sentries ready to fire waiting barrels of tar to warn of approaching British ships.

The quartz crystals are Lantern Hill's crowning glory and potential doom. Below, to the south, there is a silex mine—you can see the cut, the crusher, and the loader from the summit—which has already cut halfway through an adjoining hill. The same vein goes through Lantern Hill!

After reaching the ridge, the trail twists and turns, but the narrow top precludes more than a momentary loss of the blue blazes. The trail swings left to a cliff used by rock climbers for a view of the wooded countryside to the southeast. On a clear day, you can see the Fisher's Island and Long Island Sound to the south. If you have elected to hike the full 8.4 miles, this ledge makes an excellent lunch spot. When ready, retrace your steps to Fanning Road.

41 Macedonia Brook

Total distance: 7.2 miles
Hiking time: 4½ hours/Rating: B
Highlights: Views

A cluster of hills 1,000 to 1,400 feet high separated by pure, clear Macedonia Brook fills Macedonia Brook State Park. In addition to a section of the famous Appalachian Trail (AT), this 2,294-acre park has an extensive trail system of its own.

Macedonia Brook lies just inside Connecticut's western boundary. From Kent, take CT 341 west for 1.7 miles, where a sign directs you into the park down a paved road on the right. The loop hike described here starts at Maple Campground, located just beyond a gravel crossroads 5.1 miles inside the park.

For the first 3.1 miles, you follow the white blazes of the heavily traveled AT. Take the gravel road west across the brook and uphill. Beneath an ash tree on the right we found two morels. Acclaimed as our best-tasting mushroom, this hollow, light brown fungus with an exterior raised latticework is the elusive spring goal of the dedicated mycologist.

At the top of this first grade, the trail turns left into the woods climbing steadily and fairly steeply. In June a few pink azaleas or June pinks spot the hill with color and fragrance. Threading through the laurel undergrowth, the grade eases as

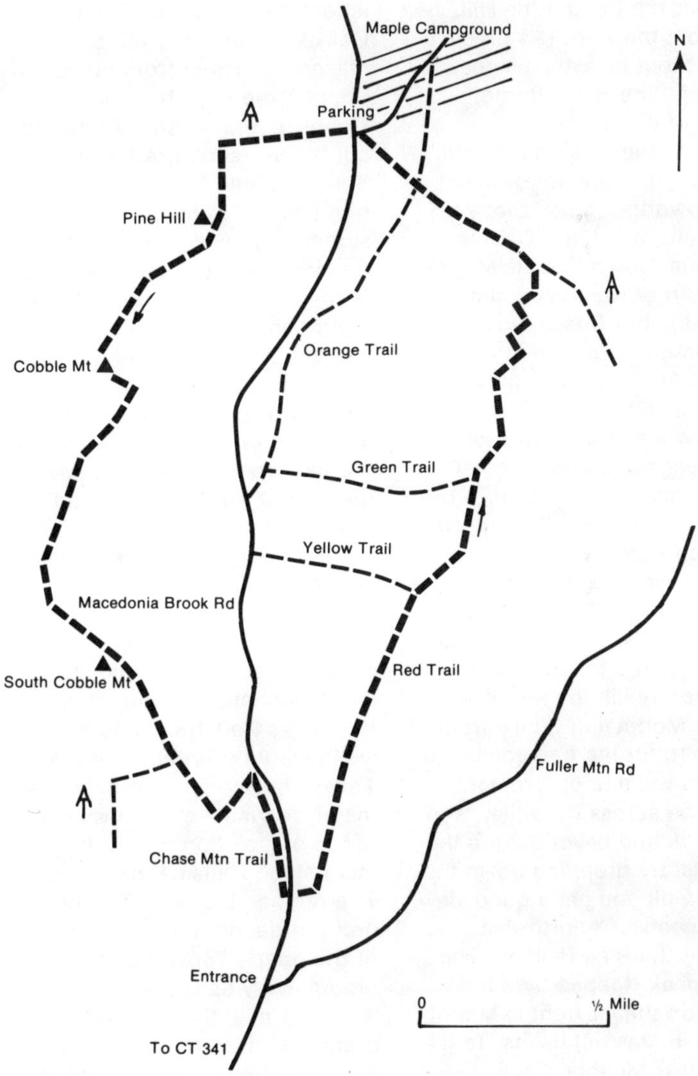

Mountain laurel in bloom

Maple Campground

Parking

N

Pine Hill

Orange Trail

Cobble Mt

Green Trail

Yellow Trail

Macedonia Brook Rd

Red Trail

South Cobble Mt

Fuller Mtn Rd

Chase Mtn Trail

Entrance

0   ½ Mile

To CT 341

you near the top of Pine Hill, .6 mile from the start. (As on most Connecticut hills, the steepest slope on Pine Hill is in the middle of the grade.)

From the ledges on Pine Hill's far side, you have an excellent view down the valley. Close by, from right to left, are Cobble Mountain, South Cobble Mountain (both of which you climb on this hike), and Chase Mountain. In the center distance are Mounts Algo and Schaghticoke (see Hike 47).

Follow the trail down over steep ledges, passing a green-blazed trail, left, in the col. Continuing uphill, the AT steepens and then eases again as it passes several large beds of wild oats with drooping bell-shaped flowers.

Be prepared for superb views when you reach the top of Cobble Mountain (.8 mile from Pine Hill), for the trail edges its exposed western escarpment. The ridge across the valley is in New York and beyond it are the Catskills. By dropping down the ledges a bit you get a good view of Connecticut's northwest corner—the Riga Plateau. The tallest peak (topped by a fire tower) on the far right is Mount Everett in Massachusetts. To its left is Bear Mountain in Connecticut (see Hike 35).

Continue on these exposed ledges to their far end, where Cobble Mountain Trail (blue blazes) comes in from the left. Stay on the AT, which drops steeply over the ledges into the col before rising gradually up South Cobble Mountain. The trail passes to the left of the summit. Then follow the steep, rocky route down into the col as far as the yellow-blazed Chase Mountain Trail (1.7 miles from Cobble Mountain). Turn left onto this trail (the AT continues straight over Chase Mountain), and head downhill for .5 mile to the park road. Follow the pavement right for .3 mile to the Red Trail, a tote road on the left near the boundary of a small private estate.

The trail ascends slowly but steadily, passing to the right of an unnamed peak. Unlike the AT and Connecticut's Blue Trails, the park's Red Trail is neither well cleared nor heavily worn. These shortcomings provide its major charms—a wildness and a sense of isolation that well-maintained trails cannot convey. The remnants of an old apple orchard decorate the trail; many of the gnarled specimens still bloom every spring.

After 1 mile the Yellow Trail branches off to the left, followed in .5 mile by the Green Trail. A short distance beyond the Green Trail you walk past several clumps of gray birches on the left. These dowdy cousins of the sparkling white birch have grayer bark that is not inclined to peel. A short-lived tree with triangular leaves and black triangular patches beneath the base of each limb, the gray birch is an early colonizer of uncultivated open fields.

The trail turns left off the tote road, climbing easily and steadily up another unnamed summit. In spring the greenish yellow flowers of the many striped maples here lend a faint but delightful fragrance to the woods. The flower clusters dangle from the branches like earrings.

From the side of this 1,361-foot hill, the Red Trail drops steeply to a deeply worn old town road (the AT), 1 mile from the Green Trail. Head left for .5 mile, following the AT's white blazes, to the gravel crossroads and your car.

42 Sleeping Giant

Total distance: 6 miles
Hiking time: 4 hours/Rating: A
Highlights: Views

Tower atop Mt. Carmel

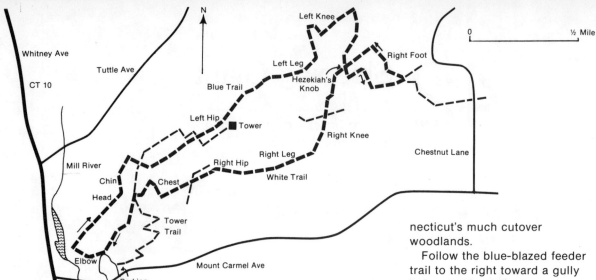

Some hikers belittle the size of the Sleeping Giant, for he rises only 700 feet above sea level. They forget he is lying down; were he to awaken and get to his feet, he would stand some two miles tall!

A series of mounded and angular hills just north of New Haven define the shape of the reclining titan. From the various parts of his anatomy, you can see numerous ridges and peaks that other hikes in this book traverse. The giant is now enclosed by a 1,300-acre state park. Only a short distance from downtown New Haven, it is a popular spot with campers, picnickers, and hikers. In 1977 the Sleeping Giant trail system was dedicated as a National Scenic Trail.

From the junction of CT 42 and CT 10, drive south 4.3 miles on CT 10 to the light at Mount Carmel Avenue. Follow this street left (east) for .3 mile to the state park entrance and parking lot. Quinnipiac College is just

across the road.

The twenty-eight-mile park trail system designed by Norman Greist and Richard Elliott, key members of the Sleeping Giant Park Association, is ingeniously laid out in a series of loops. No matter how long or short a hike you wish, you need never retrace your steps. Six east-west trails, marked with blue, white, violet, green, orange, and yellow blazes, join the opposite ends of the park. Five north-south trails, blazed with red diamonds, squares, hexagons, circles, and triangles, cut across the park. The loop combinations you may devise are endless.

We favor the blue-white combination. It is the most strenuous, covers most of the giant's anatomy, and affords the best views. Start up the right side of the paved picnic loop through the pine-shaded grove. To your right is a cluster of four great red oaks. These tall oaks did not from "little acorns grow;" they are stump sprouts from a tree cut long ago. Tree clusters like this one are common in Con-

necticut's much cutover woodlands.

Follow the blue-blazed feeder trail to the right toward a gully before cutting left across the hillside. You soon join the main blue-blazed Quinnipiac Trail, the oldest in Connecticut's Blue Trail system. Bear right.

Shortly the first ascent takes you onto the giant's elbow. The trail follows the cedar-spotted basalt ridge of his crooked arm to the right, drops down, and then ascends his head. A quarry falls off steeply to your left. This stretch is a long, difficult scramble—a good test of your hiking condition. (Avoid this area in winter; the slope is icy and treacherous.)

Back to the right are two ridges. The Quinnipiac Trail runs along the closer mass of shapeless hills; the Regicides Trail (see Hike 50), the long ridge farther right. (The east end of West Rock on the Regicides Trail offers a particularly good overall perspective of the giant.) The neat lawns and tastefully spaced buildings of Quinnipiac College lie below.

Continue to the jutting cliff of the giant's chin. The paved road in the valley below is the Tower Trail; beyond it rises the giant's massive chest. Looking north, you can see the traprock ridges known as the Hanging Hills, where the Metacomet and Matta-besett trails join. West Peak, a large rock mass with a crown of towers, lies at the left just beyond the rock tower of Castle Crag (see Hike 49). The flat-topped peak to the right is South Mountain. The city of Meriden fills the break in the ridge; the two hills farthest right are Mount Lamentation and Chauncey Peak (see Hike 27). All these basalt peaks and plateaus resulted from lava flows some 200 million years ago.

The trail zigzags steeply down the north end of the giant's head and then climbs his left hip, also known as Mount Carmel, 1.5 miles from the picnic area. The best view in the park is from the top of the summit tower, a ramped rock structure built by the WPA in the 1930s. The hilly panorama continues east and south; starting from Mount Lamentation, you see the im-pressive cliff faces of Mount Higby (see Hike 33), the gap through which US 6 passes, and the long ridge of Beseck Moun-tain. Like the hills to the north, these ridges are all traversed by trails. The barrenness of the land makes landowners more willing to give hiking clubs permission to cut trails on the hills than on

their more fertile property.

The trail continues to the cliff edge, where you can look south to the giant's right hip, right leg, and right knee before dropping down to the right. After a level spell through white pines, it drops and then ascends his left leg. It dips again and goes up the left knee. Note the pitting on the weathered rocks. Produced by centuries of exposure, they contrast sharply with the smooth faces of a few nearby recently uncovered rocks.

Working down the far end of the giant's knee, you encounter the first section of smooth, roll-ing, rock-free trail. Footing makes a tremendous difference in hiking difficulty! The size of the dogwood here attests to the rich depth of the soil.

Begin your ascent of Hezekiah's Knob. As you near the top (3.2 miles from the start), look to the right for early spring-blooming purple and white hepa-ticas with their characteristic three-lobed leaves left over from the previous summer. The leaf's shape, supposedly like a liver's, was the basis for its medicinal use in various liver problems.

The blue and white trails meet on the knob. You can return on the white trail now or continue a bit farther on the giant's right foot at the park's southern end. The blue trail describes a long

zigzag down the slope. At the next junction, bear left with the green blazes. In a few yards, turn left again onto the white trail to climb his right foot. From the summit, the trail drops down to a wet area. which you pass over on strategically placed stepping stones, before ascending Heze-kiah's Knob again.

Proceed straight down the hill on the white trail. When you reach the top of his right knee, look north across the valley to the giant's rocky left side where you hiked earlier.

The trail leads down the stone-strewn slope, and then up and down his right leg and right hip. The red triangle trail cuts across the park by the base of the sleeping titan's chest—this path is the last climb of the day! Winding up around the great boulders in spring, you hear a stream echoing somewhere in the hollows beneath you.

White and green blazes mark the route here. With a last look at tiny Quinnipiac College below and the giant's head across the way, you twist down off his chest on the white trail and join the paved Tower Trail for a short distance. The path leaves the road on the right to follow a course tucked under the giant's chin to the picnic area. At the paved road, head left for the shortest route back to your car.

43 Seven Falls

Total distance: 9.4 miles
Hiking time: 5½ hours/Rating: C
Highlights: Views, well laid-out trail

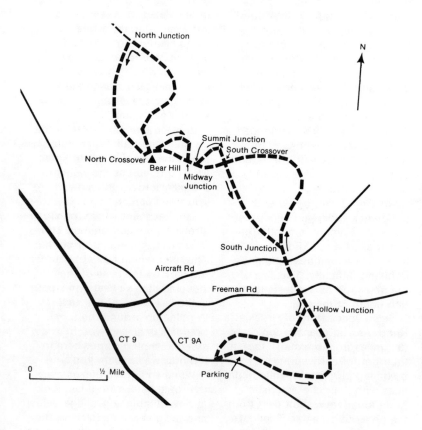

Laying out a hiking trail is more of an art than a science; the shortest distance between two points does not necessarily provide the most interesting hiking. A trail that is properly laid out directs you to the best of an area's natural features, thus offering you the finest hike possible. This stretch of the Mattabesett Trail, which starts at Seven Falls south of Middletown, does just that. The corkscrew route approaches, circles, and often climbs the boulders and rock faces that are so characteristic of the local terrain.

Another attraction of this hike is the number of loop trails. The main trail is blazed with blue rectangles, and the loop trails, generally shorter, are marked with blue circles. We suggest you go out on the main path and return on the blue circle loops to maximize hike variety. While our route follows the Mattabesett as far as North Junction and returns on several loops for a total distance of 9.4 miles, you can shorten the hike by taking only the first or first two loops for a total distance of 2.6 or 5.1 miles. This hike is far more difficult to describe than to follow. The junctions are all well signed so you should have no trouble finding your way.

The hike begins by the Seven Falls Roadside Park on CT 9A,

south of Middletown. Leave CT 9 on exit 10 (Aircraft Road) and follow CT 9A south (right) for .8 mile. The park is on your left.

Leave your car and thread your way among the picnic tables to the crystal clear brook rumbling over the series of small falls for which the park is named. Follow the brook a short distance upstream to the highway bridge, cross over, and enter the woods on the right. The blue-blazed Mattabesett Trail leads back down the brook past the falls area. About 100 yards from the road, turn left at the double blaze (the upper blaze is displaced in the direction of the turn) by a smaller brook. As we followed this brook upstream, we watched a water snake wind its way along the brook bottom. Not once did he come up for air.

Picnickers have worn an aimless maze of trails through this section; most go nowhere so be careful to keep with the blue blazes. Shortly, you cross the brook and wind up a wooded hill. When you reach the top, follow the tote road left, paralleling the power line. Along this stretch, the trail skirts, surmounts, and circles numerous ledges and boulders. In .6 mile, you pass the Middletown/Haddam boundary marker, set in a rock. From several vantage points, you can survey numerous forested, rolling hills with a few houses nestled here and there.

Two high-voltage power lines cut through the woods .2 mile farther on. Be careful at this and all such crossings. The route rarely goes straight across the clearing and except for a possible blaze on the poles, there are usually no markers between the parallel but widely separated forest walls. In partial compensation, the blazes on the forest edges are often deliberately made larger.

You reach Hollow Junction, where the first blue circle loop trail cuts off, 1.4 miles from the start. This alternate trail, 1.2 miles long, leads you back to the falls area.

Continuing on the main trail, you cross Freeman Road in about .1 mile and in another .1 mile, Aircraft Road. Climb the hill to South Junction in .1 mile (1.7 miles from the start), where a second loop trail breaks off. Keep to the main trail, which forks to the right. The path tends generally uphill at first and then heads down, crossing a brook several times, before climbing another ridge 1 mile from South Junction for an excellent view of the Connecticut River south. You cross another brook and scramble over ledges before reaching South Crossover, 1.7 miles from South Junction. This circle loop winds about .5 mile back to South Junction.

Continuing on the main trail, you reach Summit Junction about .2 mile from South Crossover. In another .1 mile you come to Midway Junction. Climb to the top of Bear Hill (640 feet) in another .5 mile (4.1 miles from the start). The profusion of huckleberries here were a major attraction for bears, hence the probable origin of the name. In about .2 mile, you reach the North Crossover. Follow the main trail; drop through laurel, climb again, cross the double power lines 1.2 miles from North Crossover, and come immediately to North Junction 5.6 miles from the start.

Now return on the blue circle trails, following them carefully. On the loop routes it is only 3.8 miles back to your car. Remember, between South Junction and Hollow Junction you follow the main trail—it's the only trail there.

44 Tunxis Ramble

Total distance: 9.4 miles
Hiking time: 5½ hours/Rating: C
Highlights: Mile of ledges

After a hiker gets his "sea legs," short, flat, often comparatively monotonous trails no longer have the appeal they once did. Aesthetic sense demands a more varied terrain, and toughened muscles, more of a challenge. The lengthy Tunxis Ramble with its Mile of Ledges should satisfy both these needs nicely. The loop route described here makes a delightful hike through the forest north of Bristol, particularly in June when the laurel is in flower.

From the junction of CT 4 and CT 72 east of Burlington, proceed south on CT 72 for 4.3 miles. Turn left on East Plymouth Road and after .7 mile park on the right opposite a gate. A sign reads "Old **Marsh** Nature Trails." The Tunxis Trail, here marked with solid blue blazes, turns left off the road through the gateway. Blue blazes with a yellow dot in the center and others with a white dot in the center mark the routes on which you will complete the circuit.

Proceed along the well-beaten tote road. A little flower whose name rivals its delicate purple beauty, gill-over-the-ground, is plentiful here. On the right at the edge of a large stand of red pine, a huge gnarled maple exudes character. The maple's twisting,

Stand of red pine

wide-spreading limbs grown over with green plants and fungi are only part of its attraction. Here is the commonplace blown up to heroic proportions!

Bear left on the tote road as it passes a swamp filled with skunk cabbage. About .5 mile from the start, turn right at the Mile of Ledges sign. This section of trail is a never-ending series of boulders, ledges, and cleft rocks. In June the faint perfume and showy flowers of mountain laurel growing from dark recesses in the moss-cushioned rocks heighten the beauty of each twist and turn. The trail crosses an old mill dam — what is left of it; remnants of cement still hold some of the angular rocks together. As you leave the ledges, the chugs and jug-a-rums of green and bull frogs echo through the humid air.

When you reach paved Greer Road 2 miles from the start, turn left. After .5 mile the pavement comes to an end; continue straight ahead on the deeply eroded old gravel road, which comes in from the left, marked by blue blazes with centered yellow dots. This path passes close to a house on the right. Please respect the rights of property owners; much of our hiking is done on private land and is a privilege, not a right! Stout-stemmed bracken fern, a lover of dry

ground, and yellow-blossomed whorled loosestrife are prevalent here.

After 1.5 miles on this old road, you reach gravel Johnnycake Mountain Road; follow the blazes, now blue with a centered white dot, to the left. The next mile of road walking takes you by a private game farm at the top of the hill. Strutting peacocks utter unearthly cries from pens. The sides of the road are rife with vegetation; meadow rue, angelica, wild geranium, yarrow, and horsemint are common, and an attractive alien that escaped from colonial gardens, the orange day lily, abounds.

After passing slightly west of Johnnycake Mountain, the trail turns left on another tar road. This road turns to dirt, deteriorates to two ruts in the grass, and finally becomes impassable to cars. You pass a pretty little pond filled with pollywogs on the right. Sweet fern and steeplebush are plentiful.

The tote road crosses a small stream; the large patch of trees on your left were killed when water from a beaver dam flooded their roots. Occasional toads and frogs jump through the grass. Short, dumpy hops identify the toads; the wood frogs make long energetic leaps.

The tote road forks 1.1 miles from Johnnycake Mountain Road

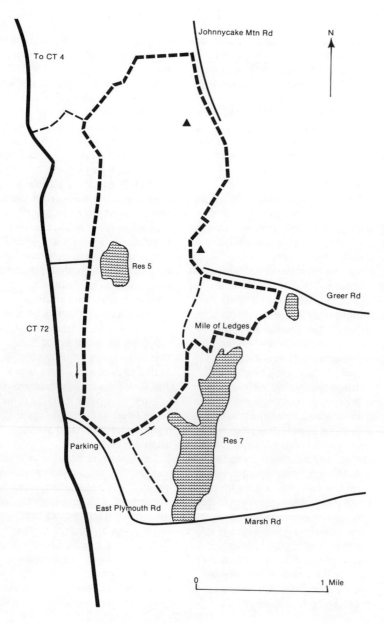

(6.1 miles from the start); turn left with the blue and white blazes. You pass a house .5 mile down this lane—you are now on a very long private driveway. One mile farther on, you cross Blueberry Hill Road and pass through a gate. Reservoir 5 is on the left. Continue straight on the gravel road on reservoir property. When the road bends left, proceed straight into the woods on an overgrown tote road with the blue/white blazes. You come to a steep descent and then ascent. Pass through the several large patches of poison ivy carefully.

The trail finally bends sharply to the right down to East Plymouth Road. Your car is parked about .5 mile down the road to the left.

45 Cockaponset

Total distance: 10 miles
Hiking time: 5½ hours/Rating: CD
Highlights: Reservoirs, very well-laid out trail

Cockaponset State Forest is a 15,000-acre monument to the Civilian Conservation Corps. In its heyday (1933-1941), this forest had three encampments with a force three times that now employed for the entire forest system. The passage of forty years has not obliterated the roadside fireholes, stonework ditches, stepped trails, and tasteful plantings.

This hike starts by Pattaconk Reservoir in Chester. From CT 9 take exit 6 to CT 148. Follow this road west for 2.4 miles to Filley Road and turn right. The parking lot is on your left in 1.3 miles.

Follow the blue-blazed trail downhill past an outhouse; then turn left on a wide, graded gravel trail marked with both white and blue. In 1977 literally thousands of chipmunks enlivened these woods. Chipmunks, like many species of small mammals whose numbers are not limited by predators, go through population cycles. From a very low point, their numbers increase steadily until they seem to be everywhere; then disease or starvation decimates the population and the cycle starts over again.

The wide gravel path soon narrows and, curving around an inlet of Pattaconk Reservoir, crosses a brook on two well-

Small dam in Cockaponset

placed stones. The rattling cry of
the belted kingfisher frequently
shatters the woodland silence.
From a well-sited perch these
birds wait for their prey; sighting
a small fish, they make a head-
first plunge into the water to
snare it.

After about 1 mile you cross
another brook where the west
lobe of the reservoir fades into a
swamp. Here the white trail
curves right. Continue with the
blue blazes for ½ mile to un-
paved County Road. In spring the
ledges in this section are
decorated with dwarf ginseng,
white violets, wood anemone,
solomon's seal, and a profusion
of mountain laurel.

Proceed left on County Road
for about 100 yards before
turning right on a tote road. On
your left is a laurel-covered hillside; on your right, a brushy
swamp. Farther on, large marsh
marigolds brighten the banks of
yet another stream. A short
detour left just beyond the
stream takes you to a dammed-
up cattail swamp. Continue on
the tote road, deeply rutted in
spots, for another ½ mile before
turning to the right into the
woods.

Just before you reach gravel
Jericho Road you pass a small
stand of red spruce; this is the
only native spruce found in any
numbers in Connecticut. Its

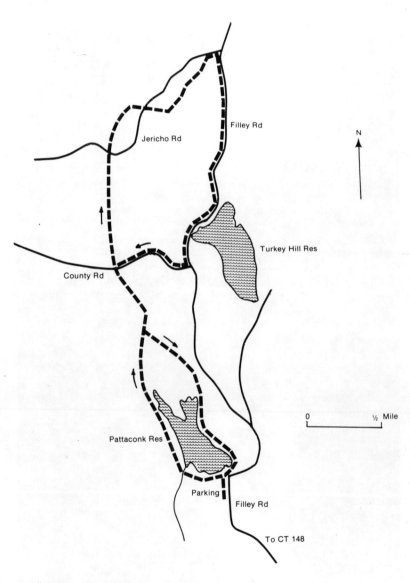

Filley Rd

Jericho Rd

N

Turkey Hill Res

County Rd

Pattaconk Res

Parking

Filley Rd

To CT 148

0   ½ Mile

needle-covered twigs, when boiled with molasses or a similar sweetener and fermented, yield spruce beer—a good scurvy remedy.

Bear right a short distance on Jericho Road past an old CCC waterhole on your left—globules of wood frog eggs may be seen here in early spring—and then turn left back into the woods.

The next mile of trail to the second crossing of Jericho Road is a work of art—trail layout and construction at its best. It is stepped, curbed, graded, and routed by all points of interest. It was constructed only incidently for the ease and comfort of the hiker; after forty years of use, trail erosion here is practically nonexistent.

The trail in the midst of this scenic mile climbs and follows a brush-crowned long rock ridge. Along this ridge are four spaced concrete blocks, the underpinnings of an old fire tower. These remnants tell two stories: the prominence of this ridge as a lookout and the sad nationwide substitution for an old institution of modern, efficient fire-spotting planes. The fire tower with a warden in lonely vigil was a favorite goal of hikers—both for good views and good stories.

After crossing Jericho Road again, the laurel-lined trail passes several low, protruding ledges patched with large clumps of rock tripe. About ¼ mile farther the trail skirts a swamp, on the left, which in spring is sprinkled with tiny, yellow spicebush blossoms.

At the third and final intersection with Jerico Road, leave the trail and follow the road right for ¹⁄₁₀ mile and the turn right again on Filley Road. About ¾ mile down the road there is a pump on your right to slake your thirst. Another ¼ mile brings you to Turkey Hill Reservoir, on the left. County Road lies less than ½ mile ahead at the top of a hill. Turn right; if you've walked this far without lunch watch for the picnic area here on the left.

You reach the blue-blazed trail you hiked earlier in a little over ½ mile. Bear left, retracing your steps as far as the junction with the white trail. Now explore the "road not taken." The white blazes soon lead you across a brook and then fork left up a hill (the better worn path to the right leads along the stream to the head of Pattaconk Reservoir). Your route circles around the northern end of the reservoir to the east shore near some Adirondack-type, three-sided lean-tos, heavily used by youth groups. One is interestingly built entirely of creosoted railroad ties.

By the dam at the reservoir's foot, the white trail bends away from the outlet stream before turning right again toward Filley Road, 1/10 mile away. The parking lot lies ¼ mile to the right.

46 Housatonic Range

Total distance: 8.4 miles
Hiking time: 5¼ hours/Rating: B
Highlights: Views, rock scrambling

The Suicide Ledges on the Housatonic Range Trail

If scrambling over rocks and boulders interests you, here is your hike. This section of the Housatonic Range Trail does not require special rock-climbing skills and technology (all those ropes and things), but it does have two challenging rock jumbles that demand careful use of both hands.

From the junction of US 202 and US 7 in New Milford, drive north 1.5 miles on US 7. There is ample parking on the east side of the road by the Connecticut Light and Power Rocky River Station. The trail heads left off US 7 by an RRR sign just before a small bridge a few hundred yards north of the station. A blue arrow on a telephone pole directs you up a driveway.

To avoid backtracking, you may wish to leave a second car by the trail where it crosses Squash Hollow Road, a left turn off US 7 about 1 mile north of CT 87.

Remember that the Housatonic Range Trail depends on the general public for its continued existence as no state forests or parks protect this path. Built and maintained by volunteers, the entire route lies on private land, and irate property owners could close the trail at any time. Do

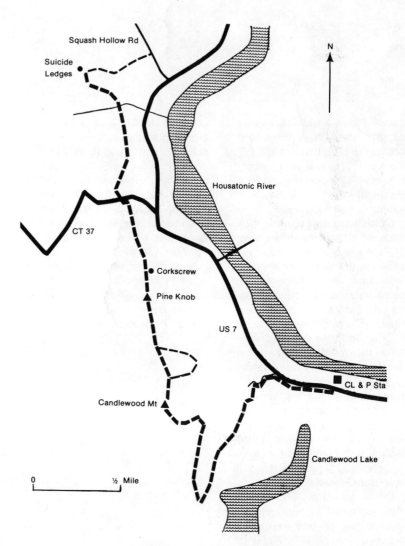

your bit to prevent this from happening by discouraging vandalism, picking up litter, staying on the trail, and greeting landowners pleasantly when passing through.

Follow the blue blazes up the driveway past the houses, and wind right on the gravel road where the paved way goes straight. Bearing left at the next fork, you soon pass a gravel pit on the left. As the road becomes rougher, you pass an obviously abandoned house trailer on the right. Continuing uphill, watch for clumps of dutchman's breeches, an early spring flower. The yellow and white blossoms look like old-fashioned pantaloons hanging upside-down with the yellow at the waist.

After about 1 mile, the trail changes direction from southwest to north by way of a switchback. Soon you go through ridgetop sprout land and cross an unexpectedly heavily polluted rivulet. We didn't determine the cause but it underlined the admonition, "don't drink from Connecticut streams." Shortly you come to a much cleaner stream with heavily flowered banks. We identified dwarf ginseng, toothwort, downy yellow violet, miterwort, marsh blue violet, jack-in-the-pulpit, blue cohosh, bloodroot, solomon's seal, and trout lily.

In .2 mile from the switchback, you climb onto ledges with views of New Milford and Candlewood Lake. This 5,420-acre lake, the largest in the state, has a maximum depth of eighty-five feet and supports both trout and warm-water fish. Continue along the escarpment. Occasional mole tunnels raise loose dirt ridges across the trail.

In .3 mile, you drop down into a saddle and then quickly ascend, climbing steadily for .5 mile to the summit of Candlewood Mountain (1,007 feet) 1.9 miles from the start. Turn right on top of the escarpment edge, which you follow, and shortly start a long steady descent. After about .2 mile a trail marked with narrow orange bars above and below the blue blaze loops off on the right. This is a very steep side trail—a ledge sloping to a drop-off—and dangerous in winter or wet weather.

Continuing on the main blue-blazed trail you reach the summit of Pine Knob (one of the many peaks in the state so-named) 2.5 miles from the start. Shortly you come to an abrupt drop as the trail descends the Corkscrew. Place your hands and feet carefully while threading your way down this mass of tumbled boulders and steep ledges. After this jumble, you proceed on a less steep slope with a few large hemlocks and white pines. Crossing a seasonal runoff, you cut left, up and over more scrambled ledges, and finally drop down to Candlewood Mountain Road, .9 mile from Pine Knob.

Follow the road right a short distance to CT 37 and turn left. After .2 mile of road walking, proceed right off CT 37 just beyond a trailer park, passing alongside a garage, and enter a flat woodland. After a bit, you curve left and parallel a stone wall. Forest succession is quite obvious here. The red cedar that first seeded the neglected hillside is now being shaded out by the faster-growing hardwoods.

Climb slowly upward through a partially cutover area. After crossing a stream, continue downhill with a stone wall to your left. You reach the great rock mass known as Suicide Ledges 4.2 miles from the start. The top of this jumble is your destination. Explore the rock caves and find a comfortable spot for a leisurely lunch.

If you have two cars, follow the trail an additional .6 mile north to Squash Hollow Road. Otherwise, retrace your steps to the parking area on US 7.

47 Algo and Schaghticoke

Total distance: 7.6 miles
Hiking time: 5½ hours/Rating: AB
Highlights: Views; Connecticut's longest, steepest climb;
  cascades; Indian cemetery

The Appalachian Trail (AT) in Connecticut offers some beautiful and varied hiking—from river valleys to ravines to mountains. This section you hike here, which ends at the New York border, is heavy with mountains (favorites with most hikers) and boasts a beautiful cascade between Mounts Algo and Schaghticoke. The return route takes you off the AT to Schaghticoke Indian cemetery and then along the Housatonic River.

The Schaghticokes are descended from a group of Sassacus's Pequots scattered by the 1637 Pequot War (see Hike 40). During the Revolutionary War over one hundred warriors joined the American forces; serving as a signal corps, they used drums and signal fires to relay messages from Stockbridge to Long Island Sound. By 1973 this once-numerous tribe was nearly extinct with the last two members living on 400 acres of submarginal land nestled between Mount Schaghticoke and the Housatonic River.

For this hike you pick up the AT just west of the village of Kent. From the junction of CT 341 and US 7, follow CT 341 across the Housatonic River to the first paved road on the left.

Stones in the Schaghticoke
Reservation burial grounds

Park at the corner, where there is room for two or three cars. Follow the white-blazed AT up this side road for about .1 mile before turning right into the woods.

The trail cuts diagonally left up a rock-laden path and continues up through a boulder field embedded in the hillside. Scattered among the boulders are ferns, wake robin, club mosses, elderberry bushes, and false solomon's seal. This is a good time to admire these plants as the uneven footing requires constant attention.

As you climb the steep slope, Kent School is visible through the trees. We once were descending this rather hazardous stretch while the school band played stirring march music in the field below. It was all we could do to keep from literally stepping off to the music.

This long, steep, rough section, known as the Giant Staircase, finally ends. The rock-free footway is a welcome relief. The AT ignores the characterless summit of Mount Algo and starts gently down. An isolated nameless peak looms ahead; continue downhill skirting left of it. Through here, mapleleaf viburnum grows profusely. Distinguished by opposite leaves like the red maple's, this shrub is topped with a clump of white

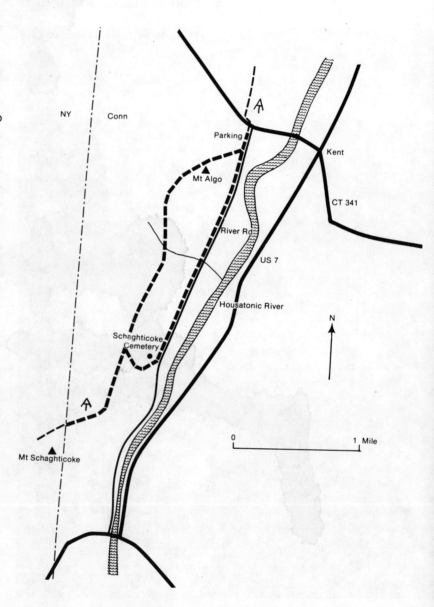

NY Conn

Parking

Kent

Mt Algo

CT 341

River Rd

US 7

Housatonic River

Schaghticoke Cemetery

N

Mt Schaghticoke

0   1 Mile

flowers in spring that become a bunch of oval, flattened purple drupes in fall.

As the trail descends, it becomes an old tote road with a steep hillside to the left and a brook-bottomed ravine to the right. About 1.7 miles from the start, the ravine begins to become more shallow; finally the AT crosses it. Looking left you see sky and hear considerable noise. Take time to investigate its source. A brook cascades over moss-covered rocks, levels a bit, cascades a second time, and then a third. Each fall is more impressive than its predecessor. Lean back, close your eyes, relax, and let the sound wash over you. The remnants of a mill dam that harnessed the brook's energy are found near the bottom of the third cascade.

Retrace your steps to the AT, which approaches a stone wall and continues alongside it. You are now in overgrown fields full of European barberry, a spiny bush covered with oval red fruit. In spring its small dangling flowers are favorites with the great black- and yellow-striped bumblebees. Only the fertile queens of this remarkable insect survive the winter. In spring, the scattered queens search out a site, build a nest, lay a few eggs, gather nectar, and raise the first brood of sterile, runty workers.

These workers then take over the labor, and the queen retires to lay eggs. This first brood raises the next generation of larger, more numerous bees. By late summer, the brood has reached its full growth in both numbers and size. Then a new batch of queens is reared before the frosts of autumn wipe out the previous generation, and the cycle repeats.

You cross a small stream flowing through the fields and then a stone wall. The trail passes along the base of the hill on the right and then cuts diagonally upward; an almost sheer rock face drops off a few feet to the left. Here there are occasional views into the valley and across the river.

You zigzag steadily upward before dropping into a ravine, where you cross the boulder-filled stream bed (about 2.8 miles from the start) and ascend the other side. Continue steeply up along the hemlock-covered hillside before dropping in and out of the steep-sided Dry Gulch. Here note the blue-blazed trail heading down on your left—you will use this route on the way back.

After climbing out of the ravine you come to some flat rocks on the left known as Indian rocks— an excellent lunch spot and lookout with views of the Housatonic River valley. Occasionally

a turkey vulture may be seen soaring below you.

Continue to the New York state line and sign in at the AT register. You have hiked 3.6 miles thus far. Then retrace your steps to Dry Gulch and take the blue-blazed feeder trail, which is now on your right. A rivulet threading the ravine plays peek-a-boo with hikers passing through. At first it is hidden beneath the porous till; then an impervious layer forces it to the surface. Later it disappears, only to reappear further on. The trail down is a riot of flowers in spring. With little effort we noted white violets, solomon's seal, false solomon's seal, silverweed, early saxifrage, early meadow-rue, blue cohosh, wild geraniums, pink lady-slippers, purple violets, and wild strawberries.

About .8 mile from the AT you arrive at dirt River Road. The Shaghticoke Reservation Indian Burial Grounds, established in 1742, are on your left. One grave of note proclaims "Eunice Mauwee, a Christian Indian Princess, 1756-1860"!

Turn left on the gravel road, which soon becomes tar. After 2.8 miles you reach your car. Varied lowland vegitation and birdlife delight your senses as you walk with the river at your right and the mountains at your left.

48 Tunxis North

Total distance: 12 miles
Hiking time: 7 hours/Rating: C
Highlights: Pleasant woods, view

You can complete this hike across Pine Mountain in 6 miles if you have a way of returning to your car from the far end. Hiking clubs solve this problem by spotting several cars at one end of the trail, and then driving to the other end to start hiking. If you have hiking friends you can do the same. One of our friends used to sequester a bicycle at the far end and leave his family resting while he pedaled back to the car.

Save this hike until you are proficient at following marked trails. The Tunxis Trail over Pine Mountain is well blazed, but lack of a well-worn footpath in many places makes this route a Chinese puzzle. If you lose the blazes, return to the last one you saw, and carefully pick out the next one.

From the junction of CT 20 and CT 179 in East Hartland, drive west 1.1 miles on Walnut Hill Road (old CT 20), a dead end. Park where the blue-blazed Tunxis Trail crosses on an old woods road. To reach the other end of the hike, proceed south on CT 179 for 3.4 miles from the East Hartland junction. This section of the trail ends directly opposite east-tending Legeyt Road. (Due to lack of landowner

Moosewood catching the sun's rays in a small clearing

permission, there are several gaps in the Tunxis Trail, including the section just south of here.)

Leaving Walnut Hill Road, follow the trail left through a forest of hemlocks and mixed hardwoods. Untouched for at least two generations, the mature trees are quite impressive. Several display holes characteristic of the pileated woodpecker's search for grubs and ants. Much of this trail slabs the sloping eastern wall of 2,000-acre Barkhamstead Reservoir, the lynchpin of Hartford's water supply. In 1 mile, proceed parallel to an old barbed-wire fence; on the other side there are numerous yellow signs warning the public off reservoir lands.

Beyond a couple of deep gullies, you cross Robert's Brook 2 miles from Walnut Hill Road. Stepping stones keep your feet dry. Watch carefully for the blue blazes along the next mile to dirt Pine Mountain Road, which the trail crosses. An easy ½-mile climb from here takes you to the summit of Pine Mountain. Although this peak is 1,391 feet high, it looks lower because of the general high elevation of this whole area. The view from the rounded top is obscured by trees, but a short overgrown path to the left goes through the brush to a ledge with an unimpeded outlook to the east.

The elevation and northern location of this area produces a climate more common to New Hampshire. Here you can find such flora as moosewood, hobblebush, mountain ash, and wood sorrel. In fact, the wood sorrel, so common in the White Mountains, is rarely found in Connecticut. The fine red lines radiating from the center of five white petals lend a pink aura to this delicate flower.

In this vicinity we were attacked by a great bustling, hissing form that charged through the bushes. A seemingly enraged female ruffed grouse was careful to veer off while still a dozen feet away. In the interim her sizable chick-sized brood fluttered off to various hiding places. Later, when we, the interlopers, had gone, she reassembled her family to continue their foraging operation.

Dropping down through white pines and hemlocks, you emerge on a dirt road ½ mile from Pine Mountain. Follow the blue blazes to the left. About ¼ mile down this road at left stand the stumps of a decimated grove of red pine. Their tops were snapped off like matchsticks by heavy spring snows. Having observed this phenomenon on several occasions, we understand why this tree is rarely found in natural pure stands.

At the site of an old beaver dam (left), the trail curves right off the road to avoid a deep washout that occurred when the dam broke. The now-vegetated pondsite is worth examining. During the many years of the dam's existence, silt deposited by storm and snow-melt waters created a level fertile floor. This still-damp area edged with spiraea and other bushes has patches of sphagnum moss and exotic, seeded, saw-leaved reeds.

Detouring off the tote road here, the trail bends down to cross the stream where it narrows. The path then returns to the road, which it follows to a junction by a small pond. At this point a left turn onto a woods road leads to CT 179 opposite Legeyt Road in ¾ mile. If you have not arranged transportation at this end, retrace your steps to Walnut Hill Road.

49 West Peak and Castle Crag

Total distance: 8.2 miles
Hiking time: 5½ hours/Rating: AB
Highlights: Excellent views

Castle Crag

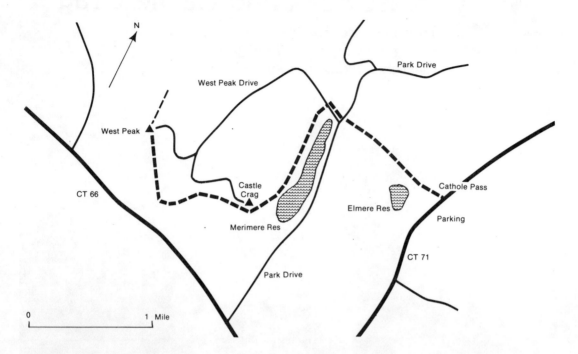

N

West Peak Drive

Park Drive

West Peak ▲

CT 66

Castle
Crag ▲

Cathole Pass

Elmere Res

Parking

Merimere Res

CT 71

Park Drive

0   1 Mile

Save this hike until your legs are working well (it's difficult), your mind is receptive to scenic beauty (the views are very special), and the day is clear and cool (visibility is very important).

From CT 66 just west of Meriden follow CT 71 north for 1.6 miles to the trail junction at Cathole Pass. There is room for several cars to park off the highway on the right about 50 yards south of the sign for the Metacomet Trail. Your route follows the blue-blazed trail left up a steep slope that has eroded to the volcanic traprock base.

The green bower over the well-worn path opens a bit as you approach Elmere Reservoir. Swallows gracefully skim its

surface in pursuit of tiny flying insects—or perchance to sip water on the wing. After .3 mile, follow the trail across the dam, cross the rocky overflow channel, and continue straight ahead into the woods. If you are lucky, you may find a few double-blossomed rue anemones on the dam.

In spring the pink wild geraniums along the trail divert your attention from the solid greens that fill the woods, shading out most spring flowers. An alcoholic decoction of wild geranium roots was once used to mitigate the effects of dysentery. Continue along a rocky, shaded hillside before dropping right to a dike with a swampy unnamed pond on the left.

One mile from the start the trail

emerges on paved Park Drive, which it follows across the dam at the north end of Merimere Reservoir. Here you can enjoy the fine view of the lake and the notch it sits in.

At the dam's end, the trail leads left into the woods. After crossing an attractive rock-bound rill, the trail edges up the long west side of the reservoir. At first, as you climb, the trail is very steep and rocky, but then the slope eases and becomes more gradual.

After 2.3 miles you emerge on cliffs that rise 300 feet above Merimere Reservoir. Evergreen-covered Mine Island below you seems lifted from the Maine coast. Gerry first saw it over fifteen years ago on an early autumn morning as the fog was just lifting. Some sights plant themselves so firmly in your mind's eye that they are always there. You may—carefully—walk around left onto a cosy rock ledge some ten feet below the cliff's rim.

South Mountain rises from the far shore of the reservoir, and Mount Higby's northern cliffs (see Hike 33) peep up at left. On the far left you can make out the jagged Hartford skyline.

As you continue uphill, several unmarked paths on the left lead to similar viewpoints offering slightly different perspectives; all are spectacular on a clear day. One last lookout gives you a view of Castle Crag. You cross a final dip before arriving at the base of Castle Crag's tower (2.6 miles from the start). Climb the tower on rusting steps for a panoramic view.

The vista west is blocked by West Peak. Sleeping Giant (see Hike 42) and West Rock (see Hike 50) lie to the south and the Metacomet ridges to the north. The white structure on one of these ridges is the Heublein Tower (see Hike 34) and the large building to its right is the University of Connecticut Medical Center in Farmington. In the far distance you can see the east-facing cliffs of Mount Tom in Massachusetts, the Connecticut River gap, and the humps of the Holyoke Range.

Leaving the tower, continue on the blue-blazed trail left across the parking lot. You cross more open cliffs and then drop down almost to the tower's access road.

Just before the road, an alternate blue trail that avoids road walking by way of a series of down-tending ups-and-downs forks left. Take this trail and at the bottom turn right on a tote road and then right again, slabbing diagonally left up an overgrown scree slope. Bear right and ascend a very attractive draw. Great traprock boulders are "flowing" down the intersection of the scree slopes. Look back—the sides of the draw frame the Sleeping Giant with his head at left.

The trail levels before bearing left up the steep side a short way to the plateau top of West Peak 4.1 miles from Cathole Pass. Follow an old road left out to a fenced rocky point. You can see the Tunxis ridge to the west from here. Several cliffs and headlands invite your exploration—carefully.

After a leisurely lunch (the surrounding thickets make nice spots for a nap), retrace your steps to the car.

50 Regicides Trail

Total distance: 12¼ miles
Hiking time: 8 hours/Rating: B
Highlights: Judge's Cave, nature center, cliff walk

The Regicides Trail passes a boulder jumble that was briefly washed by a small eddy from the turbulent currents of seventeenth-century English history. The judges who signed the death warrant of Charles I were forced to flee for their lives after Charles II was restored to the throne following the death of Oliver Cromwell. Two of these judges, Colonels Whalley and Goffe, spent three months hidden by townsfolk in the Judge's Cave enroute from Boston to their final haven in South Hadley, Massachusetts. As you stand beside these boulders try to imagine those colonial times and the people who acted out this little drama.

To reach this trail close to New Haven, take exit 59 from the Wilbur Cross Parkway (CT 5-CT 15) to CT 63 south. After 1.6 miles, turn left onto CT 10 (Fitch Avenue). Turn left onto Wintergreen Avenue in .7 mile and then left again onto Brookside Avenue in .9 mile. Follow the signs to W.R. (West Rock) Nature Center, which is on the right. An overflow parking lot is across the street. (Notice the fork in the road .1 mile before the center. You went right; a left turn takes you to the Baldwin

By the Judge's Cave

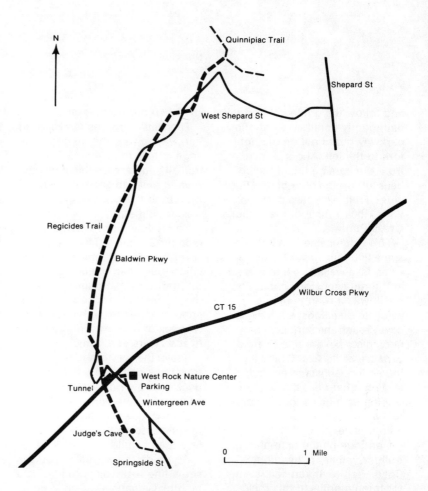

Parkway, which you can explore later by car.)

The nature center, owned by the city of New Haven, has two museum buildings, a picnic area, and clean modern outdoor pens for animals native to Connecticut. The snakes and turtles are released each fall for safe hibernation and new specimens are caged each spring. Other animals include the crow, red-tailed hawk, skunk, raccoon, wood-

chuck, porcupine, red fox, deer, opossum, gray squirrel, bobcat, and turkey. Let there be no doubt about the last two—they exist in the wild in Connecticut.

After exploring the nature center, cross the tar road and go to the far end of the overflow parking lot. Continue in the same direction on an unmarked trail across a feeder road to the Baldwin Parkway. Fork right, cross the parkway's southern leg, and follow the graded old bridle path gently uphill. In sight of a parkway guard rail on the right, fork to the left. About ¼ mile from the parking lot, at the col, bear left on the blue-blazed Regicides Trail. You pass over the West Rock Tunnel of the Wilbur Cross Parkway.

This ridge came into being some 200 million years ago when lava welled up into a fissure in the red sandstone crust. The result was a twenty-mile-long volcanic dike. Most such dikes never reach the surface, but geologists believe this one did because of its size. Gradually the softer sandstone eroded, leaving a hard basalt ridge protruding as high as four hundred feet above the surrounding countryside.

Continue on the blue-blazed trail for ½ mile to the Judge's Cave. Picture, if you can, living for three months in this rock jumble! Then retrace your steps back over the Wilbur Cross Parkway to the col and continue up the other side.

Pass an airplane beacon and an abandoned vandalized tower. Follow a gravel road, turn right down a slope, and cross the northern leg of the Baldwin Parkway about ½ mile from the col. When you pass a two-way radio tower on your right, watch out for a head-high guy wire

stretched across the trail.

The trail recrosses the Baldwin Parkway toward the western cliff edge in less than ¼ mile. The trail zigzags across this parkway several times to sample views from both the eastern and western cliffs.

You follow the western cliff face for 3¼ miles. There are several rock outcrops with clear views, but when the leaves are off, the valley panorama is almost continuous. The panorama soon changes from the northern reaches of New Haven to a series of reservoirs and farms.

Leave the western cliffs and traverse a cedar-covered hogback (narrow ridge) above the east side of the parkway. Enjoy the good views to the east before recrossing the parkway in less than ½ mile.

Again on the west side you can see a fine reservoir with a lengthwise causeway isolating a western bay. Crossing back to the east in just under ½ mile, you look out to a picturesque pond in pastoral surroundings. The dam is V-shaped inward for strength. After crossing a small seasonal stream—one of the few on top of this dry ridge—the trail curves back and down through thick laurel.

In a little over ½ mile cross the parkway a final time to the west side. Ahead is Gaylord Mountain

on the Quinnipiac Trail. The Regicides Trail ends on the Quinnipiac Trail in about ¼ mile. A right turn on the latter takes you to Sleeping Giant in 3½ miles (see Hike 42). Retrace your steps to your car.

After reaching your car, drive back to the fork .1 mile before the nature center and turn sharply right. When you reach Baldwin Parkway, turn left. (A right takes you along the ridge you just explored.) At the next fork bear left (the right leads to the Judge's Cave) to a large parking area with magnificent views. You can see New Haven, East Rock, and the harbor. A stone stairway on the lot's east side takes you down the cliff a bit for an excellent view of the Sleeping Giant. It takes little imagination to see the entire recumbent titan in the distance.